JOSEPH CARDINAL BERNARDIN

A Moral Vision for America

Joseph Cardinal Bernardin

A Moral Vision for America

Edited by
John P. Langan, S.J.

Georgetown University Press / Washington, D.C.

Georgetown University Press, Washington, D.C.
© 1998 by Georgetown University Press. All rights reserved.
Printed in the United States of America

10   9   8   7   6   5   4   3   2   1   1998

THIS VOLUME IS PRINTED ON ACID-FREE OFFSET BOOK PAPER

Library of Congress Cataloging-in-Publication Data

Bernardin, Joseph Louis, 1928–
    A moral vision for America / Joseph
    Cardinal Bernardin : edited by John Langan.
        p.   cm.
    Includes bibliographical references and index.
    1. Christian ethics—Catholic authors. 2. United States—Moral
conditions.   I. Langan, John, 1940–   . II. Title.
BJ1249.B42   1998
241′.042—dc21
ISBN 0-87840-675-1 (cloth)   97-37973
ISBN 0-87840-676-X (paper)

Contents

Foreword

It was a greater pleasure than I can express for me to welcome His Eminence, Joseph Cardinal Bernardin, archbishop of Chicago, to Georgetown University in September 1996 and to introduce his address on *The Church in American Society and the Consistent Ethic of Life.*

Just as that topic was no stranger to discussion at Georgetown, Cardinal Bernardin was no stranger to our Hilltop. His 1996 visit was the Cardinal's third to the University in recent years. He had come in October 1984 to speak on the "consistent ethic of life" and its implications for a whole spectrum of issues. More recently, in 1990, he had returned to the stage of Gaston Hall to discuss that principle in the context of the U.S. Supreme Court's *Webster* decision.

Having had the privilege of hearing these two thoughtful and stirring addresses by Cardinal Bernardin, we awaited with great eagerness his further insights. Just that morning, he had been awarded the nation's highest civilian honor, the Presidential Medal of Freedom. I remember looking out over the Gaston Hall audience and being especially pleased to have present so many students who one day would be able to recall that early September day on which they had heard a truly magisterial address.

That fall, as had been the case for his 1984 address, a United States presidential election campaign was running at full steam. In was, therefore, especially fitting that Cardinal Bernardin emphasized the need for Americans and their political leaders to oppose threats to life on all fronts. The consistent ethic, he told us in 1984, "forces us to face the full range of threats to life." It resists a "single-issue" focus by the church, even if the issue is as urgent as abortion or nuclear arms. "The defense of human life leads inexorably to respect for human rights, domestically and internationally," he reminded us. Moreover, "the credibility of our advocacy of every unborn child's right to life will be enhanced by a consistent concern for the plight of the homeless, the hungry and helpless in our nation, as well as the poor of the world."

Some call the consistent ethic a "seamless garment" or an all-encompassing vision. Certainly, it is a vision the Cardinal has made his own and championed tirelessly.

This vision underlay Cardinal Bernardin's work, in 1983, as chairman of the United States bishops' Ad Hoc Committee on War and Peace, which led to the passage of the landmark pastoral letter, *The Challenge of Peace: God's Promise and Our Response*. The vision likewise fueled his efforts in chairing the bishops' Committee for Pro-Life Activities, from 1983 to 1989. And the vision animated his later work as a member of the Catholic Health Association board of trustees and the Catholic Charities USA National Development Task Force, appointments that he held at the time of his last visit to Georgetown.

Regard for the consistent ethic was always evident in his numerous religious and civil leadership positions, and of course, in his constant, loving guidance of the Archdiocese of Chicago.

Toward the end of his life, he took a role of leadership in efforts to foster greater unity among Catholics in the United States. In August 1996, with other prominent Catholic leaders, he released a thought-provoking document, *Called to be Catholic: Church in a Time of Peril*. Decrying the current polarization of the U.S. church, it called for new dialogue. In conjunction with that statement, the document's authors organized the Catholic Common Ground Project to help bring Catholics of various perspectives together for pastorally constructive dialogue.

The service of learning, faith and freedom—in both a new nation and a new American church–was essential to the vision of Georgetown's founder, Archbishop John Carroll, in 1789. It remains no less a part of our mission today. Thus, we at Georgetown wished Cardinal Bernardin great success in the vital effort to find a common ground and offered our immediate assistance.

As a community of learners striving to live, in keeping with the traditional Jesuit expression, *ad majorem Dei gloriam inque hominum salutem*—for the greater glory of God and the welfare of humankind—we were inspired by Cardinal Bernardin's example. It was indeed a blessing to be in his presence that September day.

Seeing him then, I remembered fondly the legendary story of his mother telling him just before his ordination as a bishop to stand up tall "but not look too pleased with yourself." And I thought of how Cardinal Bernardin had made us all stand taller as disciples of Jesus. As he shared his moral vision and assured us that even amidst the fearful recurrence of his illness, he was at peace, we received again a gift of peace which only the Lord, ultimately, can bestow. And we remembered one thinker's vision of God as "the great fellow sufferer of humankind." I did not hesitate to count Cardinal Bernardin in that number as he mediated God's own peace to us.

On that day and on that podium, I asked of Cardinal Bernardin:

Please excuse me if the emotion of this moment leads me to praise you would never wish. But this audience would not forgive me if I did not say for them that we all consider you a remarkable pastor in the church, a great servant of the people of God, and an exemplary American. Still more, you are an extraordinary sign of the love of God.

We remain inspired by Cardinal Bernardin's words, his efforts to heal divisions in the church, and the great courage he showed in both his living and his dying. It is with the same sentiment that I expressed in commending Cardinal Bernardin and his 1996 address to Georgetown's community of learners that I now commend to the readers of this volume the remarkable and responsive articulations of Catholic teachings given over the years by this extraordinary man whose life and work were indeed an enduring sign of the love of God.

LEO J. O'DONOVAN, S.J.

Acknowledgments

The editor is happy to record that the original idea for this collection came from Father Lawrence Reuter, S.J., who is rector of the Jesuit community and vice-president for campus ministry at Loyola University Chicago. He proposed it to me while I was serving on the Loyola faculty. The original selection of speeches was made by Father Alphonse Spilly, C.PP.S., who worked for several years on Cardinal Bernardin's staff and who was a model of cooperation and encouragement throughout the process of preparing the book. The cardinal himself approved the project, though because of the state of his health he did not attempt any detailed supervision or revisions.

My own prayer is that the book will contribute to the causes which were closest to his heart: the protection of the life of the unborn, the reshaping of American society and institutions for the benefit of the poorest, the preservation of peace and progress in the attainment of justice, and the growth of mutual understanding and harmony within the Church.

Introduction

John P. Langan, S.J.

This volume brings together in one place a representative selection of the major addresses of Joseph Cardinal Bernardin (1928–1996) on issues of public policy and ethics. These addresses should not be seen primarily as political documents, even though in many cases they deal with highly controversial political issues. Rather, they constitute a remarkably sustained and thoughtful effort to bring the Catholic church to a central place in the public debate on issues that are fundamental to the shape and the moral direction of American society.

Roman Catholicism or "the Church" had long been a serious presence in American public life, but its strength had been demographic rather than intellectual. Animated by the spirit of Vatican II, especially *Gaudium et spes*, the pastoral constitution on the Church in the Modern World (1965), and reflecting a new confidence in the necessity and the value of speaking out on current issues with a distinctively American theological voice, Cardinal Bernardin along with some other members of the American hierarchy began to address public issues in a new way. He aimed at providing a Catholic witness which took seriously the complexities of public policy debate and drew on the resources of the church's moral and social teaching and its theological traditions in a way that invited reflection rather than commanding assent. In doing this he was articulating a desire that was widely shared by many of his colleagues in the bishops' conference, and he was assisted by a number of thoughtful theologians and staff people who advised him. He addressed the issues, then, not as an individual scholar or journalist might, but as a leader speaking from a position of responsibility within the framework of an institution that has both a rich history and a strong and continuing international presence.

The voice that he used, however, was his own: calm, unassuming, reasonable, friendly. At the same time, it was the voice of one who could be decisive, who could respond firmly to questions and objections, who was willing to teach and was unafraid to learn, who was ready to give the time required to understand and to persuade, who could acknowledge

1

disagreement while continuing the search for common ground, who ventured to address issues that were fiercely controversial, and who desired to speak about those issues to men and women of good will from all backgrounds.

When Joseph Louis Bernardin died on November 14, 1996, in his residence on North State Parkway in Chicago, he had come to the end of a long journey. He was one of two children of immigrants from northern Italy and grew up in South Carolina, a state where Catholics are neither numerous nor prominent. He died as the head of the second largest Catholic archdiocese in the United States and a cardinal of the Roman Church, a recipient of the Presidential Medal of Freedom for his contribution to American civic life, and one of the most widely watched and admired cancer patients in recent times. In his life he had known high and low, honor and the threat of dishonor, great achievement and great suffering. In the end he died a man of faith and patience, who spoke of death as a friend and who used his dying as a form of public witness and teaching for his flock and for all those who are perplexed by the mystery of our dying.

Cardinal Bernardin served as archbishop of Cincinnati from 1972 to 1982 and as archbishop of Chicago from 1982 to 1996. He was made a cardinal by Pope John Paul II in 1983. In the ten years he served in Cincinnati and even more in the fourteen years he spent in Chicago, he was the highly respected and much-loved leader of the local church. It was very clear from the expressions of grief at his funeral and from the expressions of thanksgiving for his work and his many small kindnesses that he had met his responsibilities as shepherd of his flock in an exemplary way.

But his reputation as a leader on the wider national stage had been made earlier through his connection with the United States Catholic Conference and the National Conference of Catholic Bishops, the two parallel and intertwined organizations that people commonly refer to as "the bishops' conference." From 1968 to 1972 he was the first general secretary, in effect, the principal continuing administrator and head of the staff. In 1974 he was elected by his episcopal colleagues to serve for three years as president of the conference, that is, to be the bishop who would serve as the main public spokesman for the conference and who would exercise authority over its various processes. During the early 1980s he served as chairman of the ad hoc committee that prepared the much-discussed pastoral letter, *The Challenge of Peace,* which the conference endorsed in May 1983. Since this was the most intellectually ambitious and politically sensitive document that the conference had ever undertaken, the choice of Bernardin to lead the committee made clear the regard his colleagues had for his intelligence and his persuasive skills. The process of preparing the document turned out to be more public and more complex than anyone had anticipated, and one of Bernardin's most lasting contributions may turn out to be the way in which he pioneered this new method of preparing church statements on social issues. For this method revealed a new kind of openness about revisions and disagreements and involved bringing outsiders, many of them non-Catholic, into a delicate and visible process. At the very end of his life, Bernardin also served as chairman of another ad hoc committee on reorganizing the structures of the national conference, a task that was still incomplete at the time of his death. Another committee that he chaired and that is particularly important for the issues examined in this volume was the committee on pro-life activities, which he led from 1983 to 1989.

Underlying this record of ecclesial and public accomplishment were the early formative years in South Carolina, where Bernardin was raised in a small and devoted family and where he attended both Catholic and public schools. He began his higher education as a pre-med student at the University of South Carolina but shifted to studying for the priesthood in seminaries in Maryland and Washington, D.C., where he earned degrees in theology and education at the Catholic University of America. He was ordained in 1952 and came back to South Carolina to serve in various posts in his native diocese of Charleston, South Carolina, until 1966, when he was appointed to be auxiliary bishop of Atlanta. For nearly all of his working life he was primarily an administrator, but at the same time he deepened his sense of being a priest and a pastor. He would not have represented himself as a scholar or intellectual, but he esteemed the intelligence and the dedication of those who were. He was ready to draw on their talents in the service of what he took to be the church's distinctive contribution to the shaping of public policy in our democratic society, and his speeches and writings express his intelligent and compassionate involvement in the major issues confronting the American church.

The functions of this volume are to provide a compact, though admittedly incomplete, record of an important moment in the development of the public stance of American Catholicism; to bring together for a wider audience texts that speak to the moral aspects of important issues in contemporary American public life; and to lay before students of Christian ethics and of the life of Roman Catholicism the main aspects of what Cardinal Bernardin discussed as "the consistent ethic of life" and "the seamless garment."

The addresses gathered here were delivered to specific audiences in both Catholic and non-Catholic settings over a period from 1983 to 1996. They reflect and attempt to deal with the tensions arising between the American polity and the Catholic community at a time when some widely held assumptions about the congruence between Catholic teaching and American values came under challenge and the Catholic community itself developed significant internal divisions on many moral and political issues. The enthusiasm about the compatibility of Catholicism and the American project that formed during the early 1960s when John XXIII was Bishop of Rome and John Fitzgerald Kennedy was in the White House and that had exulted in the opening of the Church during Vatican II was an exuberant and exceptional moment. It did not survive America's involvement in the Vietnam War and the issuance of *Humanae vitae* by Paul VI in 1968, which reaffirmed the Church's traditional teaching on the immorality of artificial contraception. *Humanae vitae* underlined the cultural differences between Rome and American Catholic liberals, and it provoked a firestorm of controversy that made the public expression of dissent by Catholics on this and many other subjects a routine matter. In the following decade, the United States moved to the legalization of abortion in *Roe v. Wade* (1973), reappraised its strategy of nuclear deterrence after the Soviet invasion of Afghanistan (1979), and restored capital punishment (1977). During the 1980s and 1990s, in a complex reaction to the ideological climate and the budgetary deficits of the Reagan administration, American society came to question the worth of a wide range of government social programs. Many of these programs had enjoyed a high measure of church support, and they had often facilitated the church's efforts to improve living conditions and opportunities for the poor. In the 1990s American society also deepened and extended its commitment to private free-market strategies for dealing with numerous unresolved problems in American society, notably in the field of health care.

The center of the intellectual framework that Cardinal Bernardin employed for organizing his reflections on public policy issues was "the consistent ethic of life," which he presented in an address at Fordham University in 1983 and which is included in the present volume. This framework can be looked at in either political or theoretical terms.

If we look at the positions of the Catholic church in the United States on public policy issues touching on respect for the value of life, we find an unusual profile. On such international issues as nuclear deterrence and restraints on the use of force in the settlement of conflicts as well as on such domestic issues as capital punishment and the use of government programs to protect and enhance the lives of the most poor and vulnerable, the church seems to be on the left, or politically liberal, side of the political arena. On other issues such as the legalization of abortion and physician-assisted suicide, as well as on allowing the legitimate use of force in the international arena the church seems to be on the right, or politically conservative, side. This means that persons and groups who were allies on one set of issues become opponents on the other set and that lines of argument and institutional policies which looked acceptable and even appropriate when applied to one set of issues are treated as less than reliable when applied to another set. Thus, church spokesmen will argue for federal funding to meet the needs of welfare mothers but will oppose federal funding for abortions for medically indigent women. This kind of political complexity frustrates those who are looking for either a simple condemnation or a simple affirmation of liberal views on political questions. This sort of frustration can move from simple puzzlement to denunciations of inconsistency and accusations of betrayal and bigotry. When such problems arise, it is obviously a help for both the leaders of the church and the activists on the various issues to have a more comprehensive framework for thinking about the issues from a Catholic perspective.

But such a framework will only be useful in the long term if it provides an account of the church's position that is both faithful to the Catholic tradition and intellectually clear and convincing. If it is to be convincing, it has to be both consistent—that is, affirming the same values in different contexts—and responsive to the real differences among various contexts. The consistent ethic of life as Cardinal Bernardin has presented it has never been reducible to a simple priority of life over all other values. It has included a recognition of the different forms of value conflicts as well as the different kinds of uncertainty that the church has historically recognized. The prohibition against taking life in the womb is universal in a way in which the prohibition against taking life on the field of battle is not, and cannot be, within the Catholic tradition. Consistency in the face of the challenges presented by diverse intellectual movements and the nearly infinite variety of circumstances cannot be demonstrated by one conclusive argument or exposition. Rather, it is itself an intellectual and moral value that serves as a light for the ongoing application and development of the Catholic tradition.

The consistent ethic of life is then an appropriate object for appraisal in both its political and theoretical implications. But it was not the only matter of Cardinal Bernardin's concern as he addressed the issues of American public life and the church's role in that life. In fact, the other major theme in these addresses is the interconnection between religion and politics.

Here Bernardin was able to build confidently on the foundation provided by the declaration of the Second Vatican Council on religious liberty, *Dignitatis humanae* (1965), the overwhelmingly positive consequences of the Kennedy presidency on the relations between Catholics and their fellow citizens, and the intellectual legacy of John Courtney Murray, the distinguished Jesuit theologian who exerted a decisive influence on Catholic thinking in this area. Like the great majority of American Catholics, Bernardin fully accepted the American constitutional tradition on the separation of church and state; but he strongly opposed all those who would interpret this as a banishing of religion from political life and political argument, from participation in the public square. The importance of these addresses, however, does not lie so much in their repetition of this fundamental point, but in the way they apply it to the concrete circumstances of American political life in the 1980s and 1990s.

In these addresses Cardinal Bernardin did not attempt to offer a comprehensive analysis of the direction and problems of American society, nor did he propose any definitive formulation of Catholic teaching on the issues of social ethics. His addresses are probably best seen as a faithful articulation of Catholic teaching that aims to be responsive to the changed political and cultural situation of American Catholicism and the special responsibilities of the largest religious body in the world's greatest economic and military power. They are the reflections of a man who was for twenty years the most influential American Catholic bishop, a man who led without thrusting himself into the spotlight and who summed up in his life and style of ministry many of the most positive energies and gifts of American Catholicism.

A Consistent Ethic of Life:
An American-Catholic Dialogue

Gannon Lecture, Fordham University
December 6, 1983

It is a privilege to be invited to give the Gannon Lecture at Fordham University. Fr. Gannon's life as a priest, a Jesuit and a scholar offers a standard of excellence which any Gannon lecturer should seek to imitate.

I was invited to address some aspect of the U.S. Catholic bishops' pastoral letter, *The Challenge of Peace: God's Promise and Our Response*. I am happy to do so, but I want to address the topic in a very specific manner. The setting of today's lecture has shaped its substance. The setting is a university, a community and an institution committed to the examination and testing of ideas. A university setting calls for an approach to the pastoral which does more than summarize its content; six months after its publication, it is necessary to examine the document's impact and to reflect upon the possibilities for development which are latent in its various themes.

More specifically, Fordham is an American Catholic university, an institution which has consistently fostered the work of enriching American culture through Catholic wisdom and has simultaneously sought to enhance our understanding of Catholic faith by drawing upon the American tradition.

Today I will discuss the pastoral letter in terms of the relationship of our Catholic moral vision and American culture. Specifically, I wish to use the letter as a starting point for shaping a consistent ethic of life in our culture. In keeping with the spirit of a university, I have cast the lecture in the style of an inquiry, an examination of the need for a consistent ethic of life and a probing of the problems and possibilities which exist within the Church and the wider society for developing such an ethic.

I do not underestimate the intrinsic intellectual difficulties of this exercise nor the delicacy of the question—ecclesially, ecumenically and politically. But I believe the Catholic moral tradition has something valuable to say in the face of the multiple threats to the sacredness of life today, and I am convinced that the Church is in a position to make a significant defense of life in a comprehensive and consistent manner.

Such a defense of life will draw upon the Catholic moral position and the public place the Church presently holds in the American civil debate. The pastoral letter links the questions of abortion and nuclear war. The letter does not argue the case for linkage; that is one of my purposes today. It is important to note that the way these two issues are joined in the pastoral places the American bishops in a unique position in the public policy discourse of the nation. No other major institution presently holds these two positions in the way the Catholic bishops have joined them. This is both a responsibility and an opportunity.

I am convinced that the pro-life position of the Church must be developed in terms of a comprehensive and consistent ethic of life. I have just been named the Chairman of the National Conference of Catholic Bishops' Pro-Life Committee; I am committed to shaping a position of linkage among the life issues. It is that topic I wish to develop today in three steps: (1) a reflection on the pastoral letter on war and peace; (2) an analysis of a consistent ethic of life; and (3) an examination of how such an ethic can be shaped in the American public debate.

I. The Church in Public Debate: The Pastoral in Perspective

The pastoral letter on war and peace can be examined from several perspectives. I wish to look at it today in ecclesiological terms, specifically as an example of the Church's role in helping to shape a public policy debate. Early in the letter the bishops say that they are writing in order to share the moral wisdom of the Catholic tradition with society. In stating this objective the American bishops were following the model of the Second Vatican Council which called dialogue with the world a sign of love for the world.

I believe the long-term ecclesiological significance of the pastoral rests with the lessons it offers about the Church's capacity to dialogue with the world in a way which helps to shape the public policy debate on key issues. During the drafting of the pastoral letter one commentator wrote in the editorial section of the *Washington Post*:

> The Catholic bishops . . . are forcing a public debate on perhaps the most perplexing nuclear question of them all, the morality of

nuclear deterrence . . . Their logic and passion have taken them to the very foundation of American security policy.

This commentary accurately captures the purpose of the pastoral letter. The bishops intended to raise fundamental questions about the dynamic of the arms race and the direction of American nuclear strategy. We intended to criticize the rhetoric of the nuclear age and to expose the moral and political futility of a nuclear war. We wanted to provide a moral assessment of existing policy which would both set limits to political action and provide direction for a policy designed to lead us out of the dilemma of deterrence.

It is the lessons we can learn from the policy impact of the pastoral which are valuable today. The principal conclusion is that the Church's social policy role is at least as important in *defining* key questions in the public debate as in *deciding* such questions. The impact of the pastoral was due in part to its specific positions and conclusions, but it was also due to the way it brought the entire nuclear debate under scrutiny.

The letter was written at a time it called a "new moment" in the nuclear age. The "new moment" is a mix of public perceptions and policy proposals. The public sense of the fragility of our security system is today a palpable reality. The interest in the TV showing of "The Day After" is an example of how the public is taken by the danger of our present condition. But the "new moment" is also a product of new ideas, or at least the shaking of the foundation under old ideas.

Another commentary generated during the drafting of the pastoral letter, this one from *The New Republic,* identified the policy characteristics of the "new moment":

The ground is not steady beneath the nuclear forces of the United States. The problem is not modes of basing but modes of thinking. The traditional strategy for our nuclear arsenal is shaken by a war of ideas about its purpose, perhaps the most decisive war of ideas in its history.

The significant fact to which this editorial points is that the "new moment" is an "open moment" in the strategic debate. Ideas are under scrutiny and established policies are open to criticism in a way we have not seen since the late 1950's. From the proposal of "no first use," through the debate about the MX, to the concept of a Nuclear Freeze, the nuclear policy question is open to reassessment and redirection. The potential contained in the "new moment" will not last forever; policies must be formulated, ideas will crystallize and some consensus will be shaped. As yet, the content of the consensus is not clear.

The fundamental contribution of *The Challenge of Peace,* I believe, is that we have been part of a few central forces which have created the "new moment." We have helped to shape the debate; now we face the question of whether we can help to frame a new consensus concerning nuclear policy.

The "new moment" is filled with potential; it is also filled with danger. The dynamic of the nuclear relationship between the superpowers is not a stable one. It is urgent that a consensus be shaped which will move us beyond our present posture. The pastoral letter has opened space in the public debate for a consideration of the moral factor. How we use the moral questions, that is, how we relate them to the strategic and political elements, is the key to our contribution to the "new moment." I could spend the entire lecture on the moral dimension of the nuclear debate, but my purpose is rather to relate the experience we have had in dealing with the nuclear question to other issues. Without leaving the topic of the war and peace discussion, I will try to show how our contribution to this issue is part of a larger potential which Catholic moral vision has in the public policy arena. This larger potential is to foster a consideration of a consistent ethic of life and its implications for us today.

II. A Consistent Ethic of Life: A Catholic Perspective

The Challenge of Peace provides a starting point for developing a consistent ethic of life but it does not provide a fully articulated framework. The central idea in the letter is the sacredness of human life and the responsibility we have, personally and socially, to protect and preserve the sanctity of life.

Precisely because life is sacred, the taking of even one human life is a momentous event. Indeed, the sense that every human life has transcendent value has led a whole stream of the Christian tradition to argue that life may never be taken. That position is held by an increasing number of Catholics and is reflected in the pastoral letter, but it has not been the dominant view in Catholic teaching and it is not the principal moral position found in the pastoral letter. What is found in the letter is the traditional Catholic teaching that there should always be a *presumption* against taking human life, but in a limited world marked by the effects of sin there are some narrowly defined *exceptions* where life can be taken. This is the moral logic which produced the "Just-War" ethic in Catholic theology.

While this style of moral reasoning retains its validity as a method of resolving extreme cases of conflict when fundamental rights are at stake, there has been a perceptible shift of emphasis in the teaching and pastoral practice of the Church in the last 30 years. To summarize the shift succinctly, the presumption against taking human life has been strengthened and the exceptions made ever more restrictive. Two examples, one at the level of principle, the other at the level of pastoral practice, illustrate the shift.

First, in a path-breaking article in 1959 in *Theological Studies*, John Courtney Murray, S.J., demonstrated that Pope Pius XII had reduced the traditional threefold justification for going to war (defense, recovery of property and punishment) to the single reason of defending the innocent and protecting those values required for decent human existence. Second, in the case of capital punishment, there has been a shift at the level of pastoral practice. While not denying the classical position, found in the writing of Thomas Aquinas and other authors, that the state has the right to employ capital punishment, the action of Catholic bishops and Popes Paul VI and John Paul II has been directed against the exercise of that right by the state. The argument has been that more humane methods of defending the society exist and should be used. Such humanitarian concern lies behind the policy position of the National Conference of Catholic Bishops against capital punishment, the opposition expressed by individual bishops in their home states against reinstating the death penalty, and the extraordinary interventions of Pope John Paul II and the Florida bishops seeking to prevent the execution in Florida last week.

Rather than extend the specific analysis of this shift of emphasis at the levels of both principle and practice in Catholic thought, I wish to probe the rationale behind the shift and indicate what it teaches us about the need for a consistent ethic of life. Fundamental to the shift is a more acute perception of the multiple ways in which life is threatened today. Obviously questions like war, aggression and capital punishment have been with us for centuries and are not new to us. What is new is the *context* in which these ancient questions arise, and the way in which a new context shapes the *content* of our ethic of life. Let me comment on the relationship of the context of our culture and the content of our ethic in terms of: 1) the *need* for a consistent ethic of life; 2) the *attitude* necessary to sustain it; and 3) the *principles* needed to shape it.

The dominant cultural fact, present in both modern warfare and modern medicine, which induces a sharper awareness of the fragility of human life, is our technology. To live as we do in an age of careening development of technology is to face a qualitatively new range of moral problems. War has been a perennial threat to human life, but today the threat is qualitatively different due to nuclear weapons. We now threaten life on a scale previously unimaginable. As the pastoral letter put it, the dangers of nuclear war teach us to read the Book of Genesis with new eyes. From the inception of life to its decline, a rapidly expanding technology opens new opportunities for care but also poses new potential to threaten the sanctity of life.

The technological challenge is a pervasive concern of Pope John Paul II, expressed in his first encyclical, *Redemptor Hominis,* and continuing through his address to the Pontifical Academy of Science last month when he called scientists to direct their work toward the promotion of life, not the creation of instruments of death. The essential question in the technological challenge is this: in an age when we *can* do almost anything, how do we decide what we *ought* to do? The even more demanding question is: In a time when we can do anything technologically, how do we decide morally what *we should never do?*

Asking these questions along the spectrum of life from womb to tomb creates the need for a consistent ethic of life. For the spectrum of life cuts across the issues of genetics, abortion, capital punishment, modern warfare and the care of the terminally ill. These are all distinct problems, enormously complicated, and deserving individual treatment. No single answer and no simple responses will solve them. My purpose, however, is to highlight the way in which we face new technological challenges in each one of these areas; this combination of challenges is what cries out for a consistent ethic of life.

Such an ethic will have to be finely honed and carefully structured on the basis of values, principles, rules and applications to specific cases. It is not my task today, nor within my competence as a bishop, to spell out all the details of such an ethic. It is to that task that philosophers and poets, theologians and technicians, scientists and strategists, political leaders and plain citizens are called. I would, however, highlight a basic issue: the need for an attitude or atmosphere in society which is the precondition for sustaining a consistent ethic of life. The development of such an atmosphere has been the primary concern of the "Respect Life" program of the American bishops. We intend our opposition to abortion and our opposition to nuclear war to be seen as specific applications of this broader attitude. We have also opposed the death penalty because we do not think its use cultivates an attitude of respect for life in society. The purpose of proposing a consistent ethic of life is to argue that success on any one of the issues threatening life requires a concern for the broader attitude in society about respect for human life.

Attitude is the place to root an ethic of life, but ultimately ethics is about principles to guide the actions of individuals and institutions. It is therefore necessary to illustrate, at least by way of example, my proposition that an inner relationship does exist among several issues not only at the level of general attitude but at the more specific level of moral principles. Two examples will serve to indicate the point.

The first is contained in *The Challenge of Peace* in the connection drawn between Catholic teaching on war and Catholic teaching on abortion. Both, of course, must be seen in light of an attitude of respect for life. The more explicit connection is based on the principle which prohibits the directly intended taking of innocent human life. The principle is at the heart of Catholic teaching on abortion; it is because the fetus is judged to be both human and not an aggressor that Catholic teaching concludes that direct attack on fetal life is always wrong. This is also why we insist that legal protection be given to the unborn.

The same principle yields the most stringent, binding and radical conclusion of the pastoral letter: that directly intended attacks on civilian centers are always wrong. The bishops seek to highlight the power of this conclusion by specifying its implications in two ways: first, such attacks would be wrong even if our cities had been hit first; second, anyone asked to execute such attacks should refuse orders. These two extensions of the principle cut directly into the policy debate on nuclear strategy and the personal decisions of citizens. James Reston referred to them as "an astonishing challenge to the power of the state."

The use of this principle exemplifies the meaning of a consistent ethic of life. The principle which structures both cases, war and abortion, needs to be upheld in both places. It cannot be successfully sustained on one count and simultaneously eroded in a similar situation. When one carries this principle into the public debate today, however, one meets significant opposition from very different places on the political and ideological spectrum. Some see clearly the application of the principle to abortion but contend the bishops overstepped their bounds when they applied it to choices about national security. Others understand the power of the principle in the strategic debate, but find its application on abortion a violation of the realm of private choice. I contend the viability of the principle depends upon the consistency of its application.

The issue of consistency is tested in a different way when we examine the relationship between the "right to life" and "quality of life" issues. I must confess that I think the relationship of these categories is inadequately understood in the Catholic Community itself. My point is that the Catholic position on abortion demands of us and of society that we seek to influence an heroic social ethic.

If one contends, as we do, that the right of every fetus to be born should be protected by civil law and supported by civil consensus, then our moral, political and economic responsibilities do not stop at the moment of birth. Those who defend the right to life of the weakest among us must be equally visible in support of the quality of life of the powerless among us: the old and the young, the hungry and the homeless, the undocumented immigrant and the unemployed worker. Such a quality of life posture translates into specific political and economic positions on tax policy, employment generation, welfare policy, nutrition and feeding programs, and health care. Consistency means we cannot have it both ways. We cannot urge a compassionate society and vigorous public policy to protect the rights of the unborn and then argue that compassion and significant public programs on behalf of the needy undermine the moral fiber of the society or are beyond the proper scope of governmental responsibility.

Right to life and quality of life complement each other in domestic social policy. They are also complementary in foreign policy. *The Challenge of Peace* joined the question of how we prevent nuclear war to the question of how we build peace in an interdependent world. Today those who are admirably concerned with reversing the nuclear arms race must also be those who stand for a positive U.S. policy of building the peace. It is this linkage which has led the U.S. bishops not only to oppose the drive of the nuclear arms race, but to stand against the dynamic of a Central American policy which relies predominantly on the threat and the use of force, which is increasingly distancing itself from a concern for human rights in El Salvador and which fails to grasp the opportunity of a diplomatic solution to the Central American conflict.

The relationship of the spectrum of life issues is far more intricate than I can even sketch here. I have made the case in the broad strokes of a lecturer; the detailed balancing, distinguishing and connecting of different aspects of a consistent ethic of life is precisely what this address calls the university community to investigate. Even as I leave this challenge before you, let me add to it some reflections on the task of communicating a consistent ethic of life in a pluralistic society.

III. Catholic Ethics and the American Ethos: The Challenge and the Opportunity

A consistent ethic of life must be held by a constituency to be effective. The building of such a constituency is precisely the task before the Church and the nation. There are two distinct challenges, but they are complementary.

We should begin with the honest recognition that the shaping of a consensus among Catholics on the spectrum of life issues is far from finished. We need the kind of dialogue on these issues which the pastoral letter generated on the nuclear question. We need the same searching intellectual exchange, the same degree of involvement of clergy, religious and laity, the same sustained attention in the Catholic press.

There is no better place to begin than by using the follow-through for the pastoral letter. Reversing the arms race, avoiding nuclear war and moving toward a world freed of the nuclear threat are profoundly "pro-life" issues. The Catholic Church is today seen as an institution and a community committed to these tasks. We should not lose this momentum; it provides a solid foundation to relate our concerns about war and peace to other "pro-life" questions. The agenda facing us involves our ideas and our institutions; it must be both educational and political; it requires attention to the way these several life issues are defined in the public debate and how they are decided in the policy process.

The shaping of a consensus in the Church must be joined to the larger task of sharing our vision with the wider society. Here two questions face us: the substance of our position and the style of our presence in the policy debate.

The substance of a Catholic position on a consistent ethic of life is rooted in a religious vision. But the citizenry of the United States is radically pluralistic in moral and religious conviction. So we face the challenge of stating our case, which is shaped in terms of our faith and our religious convictions, in non-religious terms which others of different faith convictions might find morally persuasive. Here again the war and peace debate should be a useful model. We have found support from individuals and groups who do not share our Catholic faith but who have found our moral analysis compelling.

In the public policy exchange, substance and style are closely related. The issues of war, abortion, and capital punishment are emotional and often divisive questions. As we seek to shape and share the vision of a consistent ethic of life, I suggest a style governed by the following rule: We should maintain and clearly articulate our religious convictions but also maintain our civil courtesy. We should be vigorous in stating a case and attentive in hearing another's case; we should test everyone's logic but not question his or her motives.

The proposal I have outlined today is a multi-dimensional challenge. It grows out of the experience I have had in the war and peace debate and the task I see ahead as Chairman of the Pro-Life Committee. But it also grows from a conviction that there is a new openness today in society to the role of moral argument and moral vision in our public affairs. I say this even though I find major aspects of our domestic and foreign policy in need of drastic change. Bringing about these changes is the challenge of a consistent ethic of life. The challenge is worth our energy, resources and commitment as a Church.

Moral Purpose and American Foreign Policy

The Open Forum, Department of State
July 12, 1984

At the outset let me express my appreciation for the opportunity to address "The Open Forum" of the State Department. I do not come to this platform as a foreign policy specialist but a pastor in the Catholic Church. Catholic moral teaching has been particularly concerned in the twentieth century with the moral dimensions of international relations. The involvement of the U.S. Catholic Bishops in the public debate on war and peace, human rights and other issues confronting our nation is a reflection and an extension of the concern of the teaching and practice of the Church throughout the world.

The subject of moral purpose and American foreign policy has been a persistent topic in American history. The content of the debate has varied, from the idealism of Wilson to the realism of Morgenthau, but the desire to provide moral direction for American policy has been a continuing theme of our national political life. There have always been critics of the theme; in the 1960s Dean Acheson remarked that there were two kinds of problems in foreign policy: *real* problems and *moral* problems. But Mr. Acheson took the subject seriously himself, and if anything the salience of moral argument in the policy debate has increased in recent years.

The 1970s were marked by the resurgence of interest in human rights issues, and the 1980s find much of the country involved in a spirited and serious discussion of morality and nuclear policy.

Both issues—human rights and nuclear policy—illustrate the complexity of a moral debate about the ends and means of foreign policy. Both issues highlight, however, that the exclusion of the moral factor from the policy debate is purchased at a high price not only for our values but also in terms of our interests. The purpose today is to argue the case for the *necessity* and the *possibility* of constructing a coherent linkage of moral principles and policy choices. In light of this linkage, I will

17

then analyze the role of the Catholic Church in the U.S. foreign policy debate.

The necessity of moral analysis in the policy debate is rooted in the character of the issues we face in the last two decades of this century. The major issues of the day are not purely technical or tactical in nature; they are fundamental questions in which the moral dimension is a pervasive and persistent factor. We live in a world which is interdependent in character and nuclear in context. Interdependence means we are locked together in a limited world. The factual interdependence of our economies raises key questions of access to resources for the industrial nations, but also justice in the economic system for the developing nations. The nuclear context of the age brings sharply into focus the problem of keeping the peace in an interdependent world governed by independent states.

The Catholic bishops of the United States in their pastoral letter, *The Challenge of Peace: God's Promise and Our Response* (1983), spoke of today's dual challenge: building the peace in an interdependent world and keeping the peace in the nuclear age. Both tasks exemplify the necessity of shaping our factual view of the world in terms of the demands of the moral order. The absence of moral vision can erode both our values and our interests.

The *possibility* of meeting the moral challenge in our conception of foreign policy is rooted in two resources of our country and our culture. The first is the religiously pluralist character of the nation. The purpose of the separation of church and state in American society is not to exclude the voice of religion from public debate, but to provide a context of religious freedom where the insights of each religious tradition can be set forth and tested. The very testing of the religious voice opens the public debate to assessment by moral criteria.

The second resource is part of the constitutional tradition, itself a bearer of moral values including respect for life and reverence for the law, a commitment to freedom and a desire to relate it to justice. To ignore the moral dimension of foreign policy is to forsake both our religious and constitutional heritage.

The participation of the Catholic Bishops in foreign policy discussion is rooted in our conviction that moral values and principles relate to public policy as well as to personal choices. It is also rooted in a belief that we honor our constitutional tradition of religious freedom precisely by exercising our right to participate in the public life of the nation. Entering the policy debate as Catholic Bishops we make use of a long detailed tradition of moral analysis and relationships with the universal Church which provide us with valuable perspectives about the influence of U.S. policy throughout the world. Drawing on this intellectual tradition and these relationships, let me summarize the position of the U.S. Bishops on the nuclear question and Central America.

The most publicized position taken by the Bishops has been the pastoral letter, *The Challenge of Peace: God's Promise and Our Response* (1983). The pastoral letter analyzes the difficulty and affirms the necessity of setting moral limits on war in the nuclear age. The letter draws upon the traditional Catholic theory that any legitimate use of force must be limited by the moral principles of proportionality and the protection of civilians; it then explores at some length the revolutionary challenge which nuclear weapons pose for the moral doctrine. Faced with this challenge the pastoral letter seeks to establish a political, moral and psychological barrier against resort to nuclear weapons. In pursuit of this objective the letter makes a series of policy judgments:

- it opposes in principle any direct attacks on civilians, even in retaliation for attacks on our cities;
- it opposes, as a moral conclusion, the first use of nuclear weapons;
- it expresses radical skepticism about the possibility of containing a nuclear exchange within the limits of moral principles.

In spite of these stringent judgments on any use of nuclear weapons, the letter did not then condemn the strategy of deterrence. The judgment rendered was "strictly conditioned moral acceptance" of deterrence.[1] The phrase is designed to acknowledge the significance of deterrence in a world of nuclear superpowers and to specify the inadequacy of deterrence as a long-term basis for peace. The conditional acceptance of deterrence is designed to challenge the idea that it promises a secure future. One commentator caught the spirit of the letter when he wrote: "In our current debate the Bishops' strict conditions may be more significant than their approval."

The pastoral was written to address both the general public and the specific forum of the policy debate. At the level of the general public, it is now being communicated through the normal channels of the Catholic Church's diocesan, parish, and educational system. In the long run, such activity may be our most significant contribution, for the letter addresses

Catholics as citizens, parents, and professionals in many walks of life. While the Bishops expected a substantial response to the letter within the Church, a surprise awaited us in the widespread public interest shown by other Christian churches, sectors of the Jewish community, the scientific and university worlds, and the national media. Attention in these circles does not mean universal agreement, but, rather, serious consideration of the arguments made in the letter.

In the policy community, the letter's fundamental contribution has been to open space in the policy debate for explicit analysis of the moral dimension of policy. As many of you know, during the writing of this letter we had a series of public exchanges with the U.S. Government. This kind of church/state examination of the moral quality of public policy is crucial to test the moral status of prevailing policy. We profited from the exchange even though several substantial areas of difference emerged—from "no-first-use" through the comprehensive test ban treaty.

The judgment of conditional acceptance of deterrence requires that the Bishops stay in the policy debate. To quote the pastoral, "Clearly, these criteria demonstrate that we cannot approve of every weapons system, strategic doctrine or policy initiative advanced in the name of strengthening deterrence."[2]

To illustrate what I mean by staying in the policy debate, let me discuss two themes which deserve specific consideration in U.S. policy: first, our political perspective on arms control, and second, the criteria we use in assessing new weapons systems.

The political perspective we bring to bear upon relations with the Soviet Union is a decisive determinant of arms control policy. The Catholic Church has had a long and painful experience with Communism—the facts of the story are woven through the history of Poland, Hungary, and Lithuania. Our history and our doctrine teach us not to underestimate the danger and problem of addressing the Soviet Union. But the pastoral recognizes that the depth and seriousness of U.S.–Soviet divisions on a range of issues should not divert attention from a central moral and political truth of the nuclear age: if nuclear weapons are used, we all will lose. There will be no victors, only the vanquished; there will be no calculation of costs and benefits because the costs will run beyond our ability to calculate.

There is no policy objective which can substitute for this basic goal: the prevention of any use of nuclear weapons under any conditions. To give primacy to prevention requires insulating U.S.–Soviet efforts to control the arms race from other dimensions of the U.S.–Soviet relationship. If we tie efforts on arms control to every issue on the U.S.–Soviet agenda—from Afghanistan to Africa—there will always be enough division between us to prevent our seeing a fate we share under the nuclear cloud.

Giving primacy to prevention of use and to efforts to control the arms race means stating our differences honestly but precisely. Rhetorical points made by dividing the world starkly into good and evil are neither honest nor precise. Such language fails to identify the very narrow but specific area of common interest which we share.

A perspective which gives primacy to control of the arms race can lead beyond the necessary hard bargaining of reciprocal agreements on nuclear weapons to one of the proposals the Catholic bishops made in the pastoral letter. We argued for "independent initiatives" as part of a policy to control the escalation of the arms race. When negotiations are at a standstill as they are today, either side can take well-defined steps which would be significant but would not mortally wound its deterrent capacity.

Independent initiatives are possible only if we establish specific criteria for assessing proposed additions to our existing deterrent capacity. In testimony before the House Foreign Affairs Committee two weeks ago, Archbishop O'Connor of New York and I set forth two criteria for making judgments on new weapons systems. The first is the specific impact of each new system on the deterrence relationship; the second is the cost of each new system. These are independent criteria but they can be used in tandem. If a particular system is found to be of *dubious* strategic value (i.e., not absolutely necessary to preserve our deterrence posture) and yet is *certain* to cost large sums of money, then these two criteria should lead to a recommendation against the system in question.

The relevance of these two criteria to existing policy choices can be illustrated in the case of the MX missile.[3] The impact of the MX on the arms race is, to say the least, very questionable. The character of the weapon, as Archbishop O'Connor and I stated, seriously risks moving both superpowers toward an even more unstable relationship than presently exists. At the same time we know the system will cost several billion dollars. These two judgments should be sufficient to require a reconsideration of MX deployment.

Other examples, like the Space Based Defense system, could be assessed in light of these criteria but my purpose is simply to illustrate how the judgment of conditional acceptance of deterrence leads the Bishops to a continued involvement in the nuclear debate. We designed the letter to have a long-term effect, and we are prepared for a long-term effort.

The relationship of moral principle and policy choices is not confined to the cosmic question of nuclear war. The continuing debate about U.S. policy in Central America raises the most profound political and moral questions. The Bishops formed their perspective on the nuclear question by drawing on the teaching of the universal Church. We have shaped our views on Central America in terms of social justice and human rights but also in light of the advice we have received from the Church in Central America.

The first truth we have learned from the Central Americans is the primacy of the local situation and the particular relevance of human rights as a way of understanding the local struggle. The case of El Salvador is typical. The roots of the revolution are surely local; they reside in the soil of long-standing injustice and inequity, in the perception of the majority that the country has been run against them, not for them. This is not to deny that outside forces are active in Central America; it is simply to say that the fundamental basis for unrest existed prior to outside interference. One can only hope that the recent election of President Duarte, a courageous and compassionate man, is the first step in a new beginning for the people and nation of El Salvador.[4]

But, of course, we are *in* El Salvador—through our advisors, our aid and our pervasive political presence. Because we touch the country so directly, there is need for perspective on *how* we touch it. To design U.S. policy without explicit human rights criteria is to misunderstand the situation we face and the role we play. To tie U.S. military aid to explicit human rights criteria is not to foist our values on others, as some allege. The purpose of such standards should be to confine U.S. military power to its very narrow legitimate role in a wider political effort for dialogue and negotiations. To fail to constrain military assistance by human rights criteria is to involve us more deeply in El Salvador without a clearly defined purpose or direction.

The Nicaraguan situation must also be analyzed in human rights terms. The U.S. Bishops have argued regularly in congressional testimony that the human rights concerns expressed by the Nicaraguan Bishops are also our concerns and should be an abiding dimension of U.S. policy toward Nicaragua. Those rights include, among others, freedom of expression, freedom of religion, freedom of political association, and protection of free trade unions. I particularly want to highlight the Easter Sunday pastoral letter of the Nicaraguan Bishops and to stand in solidarity with the principles expressed by the hierarchy of Nicaragua in that statement.[5]

While I do not wish to address events of this past week in detail, it is clear to me as someone who has long argued for a positive approach by the United States toward Nicaragua, that the Nicaraguan authorities should understand that confrontation with ecclesiastical leaders is a mistaken and unproductive course to pursue. The chargé d'affaires of the Holy See in Managua called Tuesday's action by the authorities "unjustified" and "completely disproportionate." With the Holy See, I denounce this governmental action of expelling priests and infringing upon the legitimate rights of pastors of the Church.

There should be no misunderstanding, therefore, either in Nicaragua or in the United States, of the U.S. Bishops' position on human rights in Nicaragua. What we have said, and what we continue to say, is that prevailing U.S. policy undercuts our human rights language and leverage. On the one hand, we propose to give El Salvador military aid without human rights restraints. On the other hand, we seek to use human rights arguments with Nicaragua, but we fail to provide economic aid which is needed for humanitarian reasons and would provide the United States with a legitimate form of influence in Nicaragua.

Instead, we have been using quite illegitimate measures, as the World Court has plainly said. This raises an important issue of political and moral perspective. If the constitutional tradition of the United States stands for anything, it is respect for the rule of law. This deep domestic tradition has influenced our foreign policy; the United States has spoken and acted often since World War I to build a rule of law internationally precisely because our domestic experience has taught us the value of the law.

Resort to covert action erodes respect for law—even if it is done in the name of freedom. There must be a complementarity of purpose and means in our policy. We lose both moral perspective and purpose when the measures we use undermine a fundamental value like respect for the fragile form of international law which we have in the world.

I am neither blind to the danger nor sympathetic to the imposition of an alien ideology in Central America. We have an obligation to resist this, both for the people of the area and for ourselves. But the means used to oppose such a possibility must be consistent with our constitutional and cultural traditions. Today, the face we show the world in Central America does not reflect the best of either of these traditions.

What approach have the U.S. Bishops advocated? To analyze the policy problem, we have argued for primary emphasis on the local roots of the conflict. Consequently we have resisted a definition of the Central

American question cast principally in terms of an East–West face-off. Such a definition, we believe, overstates the geopolitical dimension of the problem and tends to reduce the interests of the people of Central America to secondary status.

Moving from analysis to policy prescriptions, we have argued that the principal danger of the moment is a regional war in Central America. To stand against this trend, we have called for a regional political solution as the primary objective for U.S. policy. Such an objective means that the United States must see its role principally in diplomatic not military terms in Central America. Such an objective requires, I believe, that the Contadora process be given a central place, not a peripheral role, in the U.S. policy. A regional political solution, the Bishops have argued, should stress dialogue and negotiation within countries like El Salvador and Nicaragua, and dialogue among the countries of the region. A regional political solution requires expansion of the U.S.–Nicaragua dialogue, and it might well include reopening dialogue with Cuba as an actor in Central America. The purpose of the dialogue is to establish rules of restraint for all actors and a consensus on principles of nonintervention and at least minimal cooperation. The short-term goal of the process is to move the region away from the dynamic of war. The long-term goal is to establish the conditions of security for the status of the region and a framework in which political and economic development can be pursued by each nation in its own way. The United States has a key role in helping to establish such a framework, and we would also have a key responsibility to assist financially and materially the process of development in Central America.

I conclude with two more general comments. I said at the outset of these remarks that the Catholic Bishops participate in the public debate today because we believe our moral teaching has something to offer and because our constitutional tradition encourages a public role for religion. We also participate in the foreign policy debate because we are convinced that the major role of the United States in world affairs provides an opportunity for substantial service to the human community. We are convinced that this nation can rise to the challenge of this opportunity not only because it is a powerful country, but most importantly because of the generosity of its citizenry and the principles of the political traditions we have inherited. As Bishops we experience the generosity of American citizens in our daily pastoral work; we also treasure the political legacy of freedom and justice which is the foundation of our constitutional tradition. We wish to join others in this nation to forge a consensus of principle and policy designed to offer the best fruits of our tradition to the international community.

In realizing this possibility, the professional diplomatic corps of the United States has a unique role. As a citizen and a bishop, I wish to convey to you my gratitude and respect for your work. There are no simple problems in the world today and no easy answers. In our pastoral letter, the Bishops said of public servants that they have "a role easily maligned but not easily fulfilled." Neither justice nor peace can be achieved with stability in the absence of courageous and creative public servants. In fulfilling this crucial vocation, know that you have my respect as a citizen and my continued prayers as a pastor.

Role of the Religious Leader in the Development of Public Policy

American Bar Association Annual Convention
Chicago, Illinois
August 4, 1984

First let me express my gratitude to the American Bar Association for its kind invitation to address you this afternoon and to the DePaul University Center for Church/State Studies for organizing this showcase presentation. I would like to commend the American Bar Association for bringing important issues of public concern to the attention of the nation at large. I would also like to pay tribute to the DePaul Center for Church/State Studies because of its impressive initial efforts at sustained legal research into the complex relationship between religion and government in American society.

I have been asked to address a topic to which I have devoted considerable time and reflection during the past year: the role of the religious leader in the development of public policy. I want you to understand clearly at the outset that I do not come before you as a politician or a policy expert; I am a believer and a pastor in the Catholic Church. What I say to you this afternoon is a reflection and an extension of the concern of the teaching and practice of the Church throughout the world.

I will proceed with my reflections in three steps: (1) the moral implications of public policy, (2) the Church's role in the development of public policy, and, in the light of this, (3) the role of the religious leader in public policy development.

1. The Moral Implications of Public Policy

There are two popular misconceptions that tend to derail discussion about church participation in public policy development. The first is the mistaken notion that morality is limited to personal matters. Religious values are *not* limited to personal morality and religion. The founding principle of our society is the dignity and worth of every individual. Religious values include recognition of the dignity and worth of all people under God *and* the responsibilities of a social morality that flow from this belief. Catholic social doctrine is based on two truths about the human person: human life is both sacred and social. Because we esteem human life as sacred, we have a duty to protect and foster it at all stages of development from conception to death and in all circumstances. Because we acknowledge that human life is also social, we must develop the kind of societal environment that protects and fosters its development.

The second popular misconception is that the development of public policy is a purely secular or political endeavor, or merely economic or technological in scope. If this were the case, then the Church and religious leaders would have no specific role in the development of such policy. However, there are important moral and religious dimensions to each of the problems facing the human community, and these dimensions must be taken into consideration in the development of public policy.

Individuals, institutions, and governments frequently make important decisions that affect human lives about such issues as distribution of the earth's resources, scientific research, and technological application. Increasingly, voices echoing the concepts of philosophers and the concerns of ordinary people say that the distinctive mark of human genius is to order every aspect of contemporary life in light of a moral vision. A moral vision seeks to direct the resources of politics, economics, science and technology to the welfare of the human person and the human community.

Let me illustrate this with an example. Perhaps the most significant factor that we have to face in our scientific and technological age is that, for the first time in human history, we have the power to destroy ourselves and our world. Forty years ago the German theologian Romano Guardini wrote that the predominant moral issue of the twentieth century would be whether we could develop the moral capacity to control the power we have created. That moral issue still confronts us today with increasing urgency. A directing moral vision is needed to bring the technology of the arms race to its appropriate subordinate role. Only people, however, possess moral vision. Our hope for the future is rooted in people who can express such a vision and in those who are willing to implement it.

For example, the subject of moral purpose and American foreign policy has been a persistent topic in American history. The content of the debate has varied, from the idealism of Wilson to the realism of

Morgenthau, but the desire to provide moral direction for American policy has been a continuing theme of our national political life. There have always been critics of the theme. In the 1960s Dean Acheson remarked that there were two kinds of problems in foreign policy: *real* problems and *moral* problems. However, Mr. Acheson took the subject seriously himself, and, if anything, the salience of moral argument in the policy debate has increased in recent years.

The 1970s were marked by the resurgence of interest in human rights issues, and the 1980s find much of the country involved in a spirited and serious discussion of morality and nuclear policy.

Both issues—human rights and nuclear policy—illustrate the complexity of a moral debate about the ends and means of foreign policy. Both issues highlight, however, that the exclusion of the moral factor from the policy debate is purchased at a high price not only for our values but also in terms of our interests. Allow me to argue the case briefly for the *necessity* and the *possibility* of constructing a coherent linkage of moral principles and policy choices.

The *necessity* of moral analysis in the policy debate is rooted in the character of the issues we face in the last two decades of this century. The major issues of the day are not purely technical or tactical in nature; they are fundamental questions in which the moral dimension is a pervasive and persistent factor. We live in a world which is interdependent in character and nuclear in context. Interdependence means we are locked together in a limited world. The factual interdependence of our economies raises key questions of access to resources for the industrial nations, but also justice in the economic system for the developing nations. The nuclear context of the age brings sharply into focus the problem of keeping the peace in an interdependent world governed by independent states. To build and preserve peace in our world, the key moral question is how we relate politics, economics, and ethics to shape our material interdependence in the direction of moral interdependence.

The Catholic bishops of the United States in their pastoral letter, *The Challenge of Peace: God's Promise and Our Response,* spoke of today's dual challenge: building the peace in an interdependent world and keeping the peace in the nuclear age.[6] Both tasks exemplify the necessity of shaping our factual view of the world in terms of the demands of the moral order. The absence of moral vision can erode both our values and our interests.

The *possibility* of meeting the moral challenge in our conception of policy is rooted in two resources of our country and our culture. The first is part of the constitutional tradition, itself a bearer of moral values including respect for life and reverence for the law, a commitment to freedom and a desire to relate it to justice. To ignore the moral dimension of public policy is to forsake our constitutional heritage.

The second resource is the religiously pluralist character of the nation. The purpose of the separation of church and state in American society is not to exclude the voice of religion from public debate, but to provide a context of religious freedom where the insights of each religious tradition can be set forth and tested. The very testing of the religious voice opens the public debate to assessment by moral criteria. To ignore the moral dimension of public policy is also to forsake our religious heritage.

Who should participate in public policy discussions? In the complexity of our world today, not everything should be left to governments, even though it is impossible to ignore the crucial role of the policies of governments and other major social and economic institutions. Developing and implementing a moral vision for this nation is a task for philosophers and poets, for scientists and statesmen, for social workers and civil servants, for laborers and lawyers and judges—in short, for all citizens. Our effective involvement in building a just and peaceful world will be measured by our ability to think in terms of a guiding moral vision equal to the challenges of the world as we know it today.

This is clearly the thinking of Pope John Paul II who has said that: "Peace cannot be built by the power of rulers alone. Peace can be firmly constructed only if it corresponds to the resolute determination of all people of good will. Rulers must be supported and enlightened by a public opinion that encourages them or, where necessary, expresses disapproval" (World Day of Peace Message, 1982).[7]

In the perspective of this quotation, public opinion plays both a positive and a restraining role. At times it should provide support for necessary but perhaps unpopular initiatives; at other times public opinion should place limits on the direction of policy.

In our American society, individuals and groups are free to participate in any dimension of the public debate. This is one of the hallmarks of American democracy. However, individuals and groups must also earn the right to be heard by the quality and consistency of their arguments.

It is clear that public opinion is not always wise and well-formed politically or ethically. The task of trying to shape a well-formed public opinion, which both provides positive direction and sets moral limits for power, is central to the public role of the Church.

2. The Role of the Church in the Development of Public Policy

Because certain issues in the public policy debate are not simply political or economic or technological, but also moral and religious questions, the Church must be a participant in the process.

The participation of the Catholic Bishops in public policy discussion is rooted in our conviction that moral values and principles relate to public policy as well as to personal choices. It is also rooted in a belief that we honor our constitutional tradition of religious freedom precisely by exercising our right to participate in the public life of the nation. Entering the policy debate as Catholic Bishops we make use of a long detailed tradition of moral analysis and relationships with the universal Church which provide us with valuable perspectives about the influence of U.S. policy throughout the world. These policies include not only the foreign policy of our government, but also business and trade agreements and technological application.

To clarify the Church's role in the development of public policy, let me clarify three basic issues: the *place* of the Church in the public arena, the *posture* the Church assumes, and the *perspective* we use to guide our participation in the public debate.

Explaining the proper *place* of the Church in the public arena has most often been in response to charges that we are violating the separation of Church and State. My experience of the last three and a half years is that this precious tenet of our constitutional tradition holds a paradoxical place in the public mind. There seems to be an inverse relationship between the readiness of people to invoke the principle and their capacity to understand it clearly.

The phrase is used most often to tell religious bodies to be quiet. However, my reading of the constitutional principle—and the theology which affirms its truth—is that the separation of Church and State is designed to provide religious organizations space to speak! To put it succinctly, the separation of Church and State means that religious communities should expect neither favoritism nor discrimination in the exercise of their religious and civic functions. They are free to participate in any dimension of the public debate, but they must earn the right to be heard by the quality of their arguments. The place of the Church is separate from the *State* but must never be separate from *society*. In society, churches are voluntary associations, free to address the public agenda of the nation. More specifically, they are voluntary associations with a disciplined capacity to analyze the moral–religious significance of public issues. That, at least, is how the Catholic bishops see their place in the public policy debate.

That is why we assume a *posture* which is designed to keep our role both ecclesial *and* public. The challenge is how to speak as a Church to a public issue; how to speak from a tradition of faith in a language which is open to public acceptance by citizens of several faiths or no faith. Early in the pastoral letter on war and peace, the Catholic bishops defined their posture in this way: "As bishops we believe that the nature of Catholic moral teaching, the principles of Catholic ecclesiology and the demands of our pastoral ministry require that this letter speak both to Catholics in a specific way and to the wider political community regarding public policy. Neither audience and neither mode of address can be neglected when the issue has the cosmic dimensions of the nuclear arms race."[8]

Our understanding of our place and posture shapes our *perspective.* This perspective includes both the traditional teaching of the Church and the particulars of our present circumstances. In the pastoral letter on war and peace, the bishops had two basic purposes: helping Catholics form their consciences on the issues under discussion and contributing to the public policy debate about the morality of war.

Both dimensions have public relevance. If the Church effectively carries out its teaching role, assisting in the formation of adult Christian conscience on matters of war and peace, this will inevitably have an impact on the public perception of these issues. Questions of the limits and obligations of citizenship will be sharpened. In a corresponding fashion, the engagement by the Church as an institution in the public policy debate opens space in the public argument for explicit consideration of the moral dimensions of policy.

Let me acknowledge that the Catholic bishops in this country have assumed more of a public role in our society than was done in the past. The Church has always been active in the public arena not only because of our constitutional freedom to participate but also because of the imperatives of our social doctrine. Although some might see our more assertive posture in terms of being a "post-immigrant" Church, I would make a case for our activism based on the extremity of present-day problems. Let me cite two cases.

First, the pastoral letter on war and peace points to the newness of this moment in human history when we literally have in our hands the power to destroy life from the face of this earth. The pastoral provides a framework within which we can make a moral analysis of the critical issues facing us in the nuclear age. Although the pastoral letter recognizes the depth and seriousness of divisions between the United States and the Soviet Union on a range of issues, the American Bishops were determined that these divisions not divert attention from a central moral and political truth of our time: if nuclear weapons are used, we all will lose. There will be no victors, only the vanquished; there will be no calculation of costs and benefits because the costs will run beyond our ability to calculate.

Drawing on the same moral vision which supports our teaching on warfare, the Catholic bishops have chosen to be equally visible in our opposition to abortion. The basic moral principle that the direct killing of the innocent is always wrong is so fundamental that the need to defend it in the multiple cases of abortion, warfare, and care of the handicapped and the terminally ill is, we believe, self-evident. That is why one cannot, with consistency, claim to be truly pro-life if one applies the principle of the sanctity of life to other issues but rejects it in the case of abortion. By the same token, one cannot, with consistency, claim to be truly pro-life if one applies the principle to other issues but holds that the direct killing of innocent non-combatants in warfare is morally justified. To fail to stand for this principle is to make a fundamental error. But the moral principle does not stand alone; it is related to other dimensions of the Church's social teaching.

The opposition to abortion is rooted in the conviction that civil law and social policy must always be subject to ongoing moral analysis. Simply because a civil law is in place does not mean that it should be blindly supported. To encourage reflective, informed assessment of civil law and policy is to keep alive the capacity for moral criticism in society. In addition, our position opposing abortion is rooted in our understanding of the role of the state in society. The state has positive moral responsibilities; it is not simply a neutral umpire; neither is its role limited to restraining evil. The responsibilities of the state include both the protection of innocent life from attack and enhancement of human life at every stage of its development. The fact of 1.5 million abortions a year in the United States erodes the moral character of the state; if the civil law can be neutral when innocent life is under attack, the implications for law and morality in our society are frightening.

These themes drawn from Catholic theology are not restricted in their application to the community of faith. These are truths of the moral and political order which are also fundamental to the Western constitutional heritage. The opposition to abortion, properly stated, is not a sectarian claim but a reflective, rational position which any person of good will may be invited to consider. Examples can be used to illustrate the convergence of our concerns about abortion with other key social questions in American society.

The appeal to a higher moral law to reform and refashion existing civil law was the central idea that Dr. Martin Luther King, Jr. brought to the civil rights movement of the 1960's. The pro-life movement of the 1980's is based on the same appeal. Pro-life today should be seen as an extension of the spirit of the civil rights movement. Similarly, the Baby Doe case has proved to be a meeting ground of principle and practice between civil rights and pro-life advocates. The common ground is as yet not sufficiently explored, but there is significant potential for development in this area.

As I conclude this second part of my presentation which dealt with the Church's role in the development of public policy, I wish to repeat something I said earlier. I am not suggesting that religious groups should expect or be given special treatment regarding their involvement in the public sphere. We should earn a hearing in the public debate by the quality of our analysis and the consistency of our argument. I am convinced that the moral dimension of our public life is a topic which people inside and outside religious communities are concerned about. If we can demonstrate how a moral vision enriches the choices and the challenges which confront us as a nation, then consideration will be given to the moral factor in every policy debate.

3. The Role of the Religious Leader in Public Policy Development

From what I have already said, it should be clear that the Catholic bishop's role in the development of public policy is an extension of his teaching role in the Church, always within the framework of our Catholic tradition and in union with the Pope and other bishops. Because of differences in ecclesial structure, the role of other religious leaders may take a somewhat different shape.

What I would like to share with you in this third section of my presentation is based on my own experience of the last few years, my experience as a religious leader engaged in discussions relating to public policy. Three of my reflections will focus on problem areas and the last will explain the primary source of my motivation and energies.

One of the problems that religious leaders have to face continually is the question of credibility. Some people ignore what we say simply because they perceive us as operating outside our own area of expertise when we make statements regarding public policy. I am not arguing that we have the definitive answers to complex questions or that we have the same kind of competence as foreign policy experts. We do bring a dimension to the discussion that is proper to our competence, however. We merely ask that people evaluate our arguments on their merits. Members of the American Bar Association know what it means to get a fair hearing of your case!

A second problem that religious leaders face is our personal limitation as we attempt to develop the moral dimension of any issue. I am simply Joseph Bernardin—nothing less, nothing more. I have my own blind spots. I have my own doubts. At times I lack the courage to set forth my convictions clearly and without hesitation. Sometimes I simply do not know what to do. Perhaps you have similar experiences in your professional and personal lives.

A key solution is to engage in frequent dialogue with others—with experts in various fields, with respected colleagues, with trusted advisors. The pastoral letter on peace and war was conceived and brought to full term in a process of dialogue. While this was not the first time the bishops have consulted with others in preparing a pastoral statement, none has involved such an open, broad, inter-disciplinary exchange. The bishops debated the contents of the letter in small groups and in general sessions. We collected expert testimony and suggestions from hundreds of people.

A corollary of this is that our participation in the public policy debate does not mean that one person or one church or one scholarly community or one think tank has all the answers. Through our participation in dialogue we can share our competencies and God-given personal resources while compensating for our weaknesses and personal limitations. Our collaboration helps ensure the quality of a moral vision for this nation and make it both credible and worthy of implementation.

A third problem that religious leaders have to face when they engage in public policy development is the pressure that special interest groups bring to bear on the process. I have great respect for people who commit their talents and energies to specific projects that impact in significant ways on public policy discussions. But as a religious leader, I find that I have to keep within my perspective the whole range of issues that affect the quality of human life. Although I may focus my personal resources from time to time on a particular area, it is part of my responsibility as a bishop to keep all these issues in broader perspective and choose prudently and wisely which ones to address at a particular time. This task continues to stretch me. At the same time it can disappoint those who expect a bishop to agree with them on every idea and strategy or who expect a religious leader to be available full time for a particular project.

Two of my goals during the past year have been (1) outlining the case for the development of a consistent ethic of life and (2) bringing together under the umbrella of such an ethic individuals and groups who are focusing their energies on a particular area of moral concern. Whether or not I will be successful with regard to the second goal remains to be seen.

With regard to the consistent ethic of life, I am arguing for linking such moral issues as genetics, abortion, capital punishment, modern warfare and the care of the terminally ill. Admittedly, these are all distinct problems, enormously complicated, and deserving individual treatment. No single answer and no simple response will solve them.

The purpose of proposing a consistent ethic of life is to argue that success on any one of the issues threatening life requires a concern for the broader attitude in society about respect for human life. Attitude is the place to root an ethic of life. Change of attitude in turn can lead to change of policies and practices in our society.

These are three problems that religious leaders face in my experience, and I have indicated how I am going about resolving these in my own life and ministry.

I must make a final point because it is so central to me personally and to my ministry. There is another reality which I want to share with you—one that is deeper and more powerful than all the rest, one that is the primary source of my motivation and energies. And that is prayer.

In prayer we discover not only God, but our own true selves and one another as well. Through prayer and reflection on the Scriptures, we come to know God as one who cares about this world and about each of us. We come to know and appreciate His plan for us: that we live in peace, harmony, and unity with one another. We come to understand more deeply how all the inhabitants of this planet are our sisters and brothers, including in a special way the poor, the needy, and the oppressed.

That is why I believe with all my mind and heart that we must be men and women of prayer. Our best efforts—no matter how well thought out and brilliantly executed—will not quite reach the mark unless they flow from minds and hearts that are at peace with themselves, and are motivated and energized by values which are rooted in our religious tradition. In this talk I have emphasized the need to bring moral and religious dimensions to bear on the development of public policy. I conclude by stating simply that to do this credibly and with integrity we ourselves must be influenced by those same moral and religious values.

That is why prayer is so important for me—and for you!

Religion and Politics: Stating the Principles and Sharpening the Issues

Woodstock Forum—Georgetown University
October 25, 1984

I am grateful to the Woodstock Theological Center and Georgetown University for sponsoring this forum dedicated to the memory of Father John Courtney Murray, S.J. His intellectual legacy to the Church in the United States needs to be recalled regularly lest we forget what he taught us. My lecture this evening will honor Father Murray's memory by drawing heavily on his theology.

My topic is religion and politics. Under this heading, I intend to speak to the issues of the day without being consumed by the problems of the moment. The theme of religion and politics has been part of Western culture since Christianity first appeared in the Roman world. The attention given the specific issues in this presidential election year sharpens the edge of the questions, but the problems themselves are not entirely new. I hope to keep a sense of both historical perspective and contemporary relevance as I address three questions: (1) the relationship of religion and politics; (2) the transition from theology to policy; and (3) public morality and personal choice.

I. Religion and Politics: Continuity and Change

From Washington's first inaugural to Lincoln's second inaugural, from the Declaration of Independence to the decisive issues of this election, the themes of religion, morality and politics are woven through the American experience. Intellectually and politically, the key question in every stage of the American civil experiment has not been *whether* these themes should be discussed but *how* to structure the debate for the welfare of the Church and the State.

No single figure in American history has had a greater impact on how Catholics conceive of the relationship between religion and politics than John Courtney Murray.[9] It is now almost a quarter of a century since he wrote *We Hold These Truths*, and it is exactly twenty years since his landmark essay, "The Problem of Religious Freedom," was published in *Theological Studies*. The intervening years have demonstrated the wisdom of his thinking.

Father Murray would be the first to warn theologians against the fallacy of "archaism"—his characteristically elegant way of describing how people keep repeating the formulae of the past when the need is to reverence the tradition by renewing it. As I look at the question of religion and politics in 1984, there are some truths Murray held which need to be reaffirmed today. There are also some issues in our present debate which he did *not* address.

Murray's lasting contribution was that he provided the Church with a theological understanding of its role in a democracy and offered society a philosophical grounding for religious pluralism.

Murray was convinced that the Catholic tradition could learn from and contribute to the American democratic experiment. To facilitate this exchange, he took on the task of being the "theologian of the First Amendment." "Separation of Church and State" is the phrase often invoked to explain religion and politics in the United States. Murray believed deeply in the political wisdom of the separation clause, but he resisted all efforts to transform the separation of Church and State into the division of religion and politics.

The separation clause has a crucial but limited meaning: it holds that religious institutions are to expect neither discrimination nor favoritism in the exercise of their civic and religious responsibilities. The separation intended is that of the Church as an institution from the State as an institution. It was never intended to separate the Church from the wider society or religion from culture.

The purpose of the First Amendment, Murray taught us, was not to silence the religious voice but to free religion from State control so that moral/religious values and principles could be taught and cultivated in the wider society. This left religious institutions with the kind of influence they should have in civil society—moral influence. We are not to be or to be seen as one more interest group, but we are free to teach and preach a moral vision designed to influence the laws and institutions of society. The First Amendment guaranteed religious institutions the right to be heard in the public debate. Their influence in the public arena would depend upon the quality of their contributions to the wider civil conversation.

In the United States civil discourse is structured by religious pluralism. The condition of pluralism, wrote Murray, is the coexistence in one society of groups holding divergent and incompatible views with regard to religious questions. The genius of American pluralism, in his view, was that it provided for the religious freedom of each citizen and every faith. However, it did not purchase tolerance at the price of expelling religious and moral values from the public life of the nation. The goal of the American system is to provide space for a religious substance in society but not a religious State.

Today, when our public debate on religion and politics is particularly intense and, at times, slightly unruly, Murray's writings remind us of the value of religious pluralism and the fragile framework which holds it together.

Murray would have welcomed the vocal debate in our nation about religion, morality and politics. But he would have reminded politicians and preachers that the way we conduct our debate is as important as what we say. There is a legitimate secularity of the political process and there is a legitimate role for religious and moral discourse in our nation's life. The dialogue which keeps both alive must be a careful conversation which seeks neither to transform secularity into secularism nor to change the religious role into religiously dominated public discourse.

If he were with us tonight, Murray would find the context of the public debate different from that which existed when he wrote *We Hold These Truths*. That book appeared during the 1960 election year. That campaign surely had its share of religion and politics, but the 1980s have produced both new issues and new actors not experienced nor analyzed by Murray.

First, a central theme in Murray's work is the imperative of providing a moral foundation for public policy, law and the institutions of democracy. Religious tolerance cannot be purchased at the price of a moral vacuum. A society stands in need of a public consensus which "furnishes the premise of a people's action in history and defines the larger aims which that action seeks in internal affairs and in external relations" (*We Hold These Truths*, p. 10).

Murray's writings ranged across the theory and practice of shaping a moral consensus in a pluralistic democracy. But he never once wrote about the abortion question—an issue which most dramatically symbolizes the encounter of religion, morality and politics in American life today.

I shall return to the subject of abortion later; here I only point out that, on this issue, Murray offers little concrete guidance.

Second, Murray never analyzed what is today called the "Religious Right" because it was not a factor in the 1960s. Today, the evangelical churches which comprise this phenomenon are central actors in the interaction of religion and politics. I use the phrase descriptively not pejoratively. The premises of the movement are grounded in a particular scriptural interpretation of life. Moreover, its conclusions are solidly located on the right of the American political spectrum. If Murray had confronted the Religious Right, I think he would have done three things: defended its right to speak; differed with its doctrine of Church and State; and criticized its moral vision.

These points are worth pursuing. Some commentators associate the Catholic Bishops and the Religious Right because both oppose the *Roe v. Wade* decision of the Supreme Court on abortion. Both do oppose abortion, but they differ in both ecclesial style and moral substance on a range of issues. I specify these differences not to be contentious or divisive; indeed, I want to acknowledge that the issues of personal morality and family morality which have impelled evangelical churches into the public arena need attention. But specifying differences in approach and carefully distinguishing issues will highlight some crucial principles of religion and politics in the United States.

Murray spent a substantial amount of time and effort defending the Church's right to speak in the public arena. But he also stressed the limits of the religious role in that arena. Today religious institutions, I believe, must reaffirm their rights and recognize their limits. My intent is not, of course, to produce a passive Church or a purely private vision of faith. The limits relate not to *whether* we enter the public debate but *how* we advocate a public case. From Murray, I have learned to respect the *complexity* of public issues and recognize the legitimate *secularity* of the public debate.

While defending the right of the Religious Right to speak, I also think all of us in the religious community need to be tested and to test each other on how we address public questions.

The test of *complexity* is one we all must face; it is one the Religious Left has often failed and thereby paved the way for the Religious Right. From issues of defense policy through questions of medical ethics to issues of social policy, the moral dimensions of our public life are interwoven with empirical judgments where honest disagreement exists. I do not believe, however, that empirical complexity should silence or paralyze religious/moral analysis and advocacy of issues. But we owe the public a careful accounting of how we have come to our moral conclusions.

I sympathize with those voices who found the Catholic bishops' pastoral letter on the nuclear arms issue long and dense, but I could not agree to a shorter, simplified letter which failed to justify our criticism of the arms race and certain elements of U.S. policy.

The *secularity* of the public debate poses a different test. I stand with Murray in attributing a public role to religion and morality in our national life. But I also stand with him in the conviction that religiously rooted positions must somehow be translated into language, arguments and categories which a religiously pluralistic society can agree on as the moral foundation of key policy positions.

In both their style of analysis and their mode of argument, the Religious Right, at times, fails to address the complexity of our policy agenda and the legitimate secular quality of our public discourse. On both counts, I find key differences between the Catholic view of religion and politics and the prevailing tenor of some of our contemporary debates.

Another difference is the framework of moral vision we use, even when we come to a conclusion similar to that of the Religious Right, such as our opposition to abortion. I have argued previously, and this evening will argue again, two points: the centrality of the abortion question in our national life and the need to situate a firm, unyielding opposition to abortion within a wider framework of respect for life on many fronts. This broader moral argument is different in tone, scope and substance from the Religious Right's approach to public policy.

II. From Theology to Policy: The Logic of the Life Issues

Thus far, I have principally concentrated on *how* religion and politics should be related. But the issues of a religiously pluralistic society go beyond procedural questions. The *substance* of the religious/moral vision which the Church brings to the policy debate ultimately determines its impact in the public arena.

The sources of the contemporary interest in religion, morality and politics lie in substantive questions. As a society, we are increasingly confronted with a range of issues which have undeniable moral dimensions. It is not possible to define, debate or decide these policy issues without addressing explicitly their moral character. The issues span the spectrum of life from conception to death, and they bear upon major segments of our domestic and foreign policy.

Two characteristics of American society which intensify the moral urgency of this range of issues are the global impact of our policies and the technological character of our culture. The role of human rights in U.S. foreign policy, for example, has specific consequences each day for people from Eastern Europe through Southern Africa, from South America to Asia. But the formulation of a human rights policy is not a purely political or technical question. It requires sustained moral analysis from case to case.

Even more strikingly, the pervasive influence of technological change—transforming everything from medical science to military strategy—poses questions which are fundamental and moral in character, not merely technical or tactical. In the last two generations we have cracked the genetic code and smashed the atom. Neither event nor the revolution they symbolize can be understood apart from moral analysis.

It is significant, I think, that Pope John Paul II's approach to both medical ethics and nuclear policy is invariably placed in the larger context of the relationship of technology, politics and ethics. The interaction of these three forces has, I believe, driven the question of religion and politics to the forefront of discussion. We have not simply chosen to discuss these themes; they have been forced upon us.

It is precisely this sense that human life can be threatened or enhanced along a broad spectrum of issues that moved me nearly a year ago at Fordham University to call for a "consistent ethic of life." I proposed a consistent ethic or "seamless garment" approach as a framework for dialogue within the Church and the wider society. My purpose was to highlight the diverse issues touching the dignity and quality of life today. I also wanted to indicate the resources of the Catholic theological vision which are available to address the wide range of moral issues in a systematic, sustained fashion. The discussion which I urged last year has been vigorously pursued within the Church as well as in the press and other circles.

A key concept in the formulation of a consistent ethic is an analogical understanding of issues which recognizes certain thematic ideas among them and is still capable of identifying the specific character of each problem along the spectrum of life. Such a vision pushes the moral, legal and political debate beyond an "ad hoc" or "single issue" focus, setting our moral discussion in a broader context of concern for human life in diverse situations.

The purpose of this proposal, I wish to emphasize, has *not* been to downgrade the significance of a specific issue—whether it be abortion or nuclear arms—but to increase awareness of the multiple ways in which our attitudes or actions on a given problem can set a precedent or establish practices which influence other choices. The "seamless garment" does not equate all issues or subsume the moral problem of protecting and promoting life into one proposition. Rather, its objective is to sharpen our moral sensitivity and to expand the intellectual framework for debate on the life issues.

A year ago at Fordham, I invited a quest for consensus within the Church on the validity and logic of a consistent ethic. Tonight I am more convinced than ever that the ethic of the seamless garment is the best analytical setting in which to develop a posture in defense of human life. We obviously do not have a consensus on this point at present—even within the Church. But the framework of the consistent ethic does engage many who disagree on specific conclusions. John Courtney Murray once said that we can argue about an issue only on the basis of a certain agreement. I think the consistent ethic can provide the framework of Catholic moral teaching in light of which discussion about priorities, policies and cases can occur. I have found such solid support for the idea of the seamless garment that I shall continue to pursue its development and implementation.

It is not sufficient in this lecture simply to state the purpose and intent of the consistent ethic of life. The specific relationship among the issues must also be explored. A consistent moral vision should begin with the initiation of life. The Catholic moral tradition anchors its ethic of life in its teaching on abortion.

Few moral questions have such a sustained and extensive history. The opposition to abortion reaches from the *Didache* in the first Christian century[10] to the statements of Pope John Paul II and documents of our own episcopal conference in the 1980s. The antiquity of the tradition reflects the abiding concern of the Church for this question. Abortion anchors a consistent ethic because the unborn child symbolizes the fundamental challenge innocent life poses for individuals and society at every stage of human development. The very vulnerability of the unborn tests our moral vision, for the moral quality of any society is measured not by how it treats the powerful but how it respects the claims of the powerless.

Abortion violates two central tenets of the Christian moral vision. It is a direct attack on innocent life. It is also a failure to observe the command that we love the least among us. In the words of Pope John Paul II, abortion strikes "at the whole moral order." It attacks the moral order, not just one religious perspective about morality. Protecting innocent life from direct attack is a fundamental human and moral imperative, not an exclusively Catholic belief.

Many in our country wonder why the Catholic Bishops have taken such a visible and vocal stand on abortion. We simply have no choice. In the face of 1.5 million abortions a year, as a nation we must acknowledge that the principle of protecting innocent life from direct attack is being systematically eroded. The moral order *is* threatened. We cannot be passive when the unborn die without anyone to speak on their behalf and without legal recourse. Nor can we allow the moral principle protecting innocent life to be subordinated to other claims because the consequences of such a process would not be confined to abortion.

To illustrate the stakes at work in this question, the seamless garment approach consciously connects the issues of war and abortion. The cases are not identical, but they are related. The Catholic moral tradition has allowed the taking of life as a last resort in well-defined circumstances of national defense, but it has never sanctioned the direct taking of innocent life in war. This remains true today. From the courageous article of Father John Ford, S.J., opposing the practice of obliteration bombing in World War II[11] to the pastoral letter, *The Challenge of Peace*, which prohibits retaliatory strikes on civilian centers, the Catholic tradition has drawn an unyielding line against killing the innocent.

War and abortion are linked at the level of moral principle. They are also comparable questions in terms of national policy. As citizens of this nation, we face the responsibility of a policy of abortion on demand. We also face the reality of living in one of the two nations in the world which can initiate the nuclear cataclysm and perhaps the Nuclear Winter. I am convinced that the bishops and the Church as a whole must be equally engaged in both issues.

The policy of abortion on demand needs to be resisted and reversed. But this does not mean the nuclear question can be ignored or relegated to a subordinate status. The only "cure" for the nuclear threat is to prevent any use of nuclear weapons. We are not confronting a hypothetical or speculative future danger. The possibility of nuclear war is a clear and present danger. The dynamic of the arms race feeds the danger. The prevailing situation of both superpowers—proceeding with major weapons increases and no negotiations in progress—is a grave concern to all of us.

The value of the framework of a consistent ethic is that it forces us to face the full range of threats to life. It resists a "one issue" focus by the Church, even when the urgent issue is abortion or nuclear arms.

Indeed, the consistent ethic makes other connections among the life issues. It joins the duty to protect human life with the responsibility of promoting the dignity of each human person. The particular linkage which illustrates how these two duties relate is that of abortion and poverty. The Catholic position on abortion requires—by the law of logic and the law of love—a social vision which joins the right to life to the promotion of a range of other rights: nutrition, health care, employment and housing. The defense of human life leads inexorably to respect for human rights, domestically and internationally.

In the past year, some have questioned whether the linkage of the right to life with other human rights may unintentionally dilute our stand against abortion. On both moral and social grounds, I believe precisely the opposite. The credibility of our advocacy of every unborn child's right to life will be enhanced by a consistent concern for the plight of the homeless, the hungry and helpless in our nation, as well as the poor of the world.

Precisely because the unborn child represents the weakest member of our human community, there is an objective link to be made between unborn life and the lives of others who live defenseless at the margin of our society. A crucial challenge in raising awareness about abortion is that of enhancing the ability of people to "see" the fetus as a person deserving respect. A related challenge is that of helping us "see" all the other defenseless human beings who command our attention.

The statistics of our national life tell their story, but they are not easily seen. I hear the statistics of an increasing incidence of poverty, of 35 million people living below the poverty level. I hear the specific plight of women in poverty and of minorities, and it is like hearing the statistic of 1.5 million abortions. The statistics are *real*, and the people behind them are *real*! But if we do not "see" them as persons who lay claim on our consciences and our resources as a society, the reality has not penetrated our lives. The Church is called to help us "see" the different ways in which life is taken or threatened today. The Church needs to work with all others in a concerted effort to "see" the helpless among us. Here, I would point out that the media have a special responsibility in framing a correct vision of life in our society.

A consistent ethic is a social ethic; it joins the need for personal moral vision to the need for a just and compassionate social policy. We face today a curious paradox in our society: Some groups assert a positive role for the State on a range of socio-economic rights but want a neutral State on abortion. Others seemingly see the social role of the State as exhausted when the child is born. A compassionate society must be capable of caring for the human person before and after birth. The State has responsibilities both to protect human life and to promote the dignity of each citizen, especially the least among us. We will not be a just society until civil law protects the right to life of each person, particularly the unborn child. We will not be a compassionate society until public policy and the private sector overcome the dangerous differences separating the rich and poor in our nation.

III. Public Morality and Personal Choice: Connection and Complexity

All three of these issues—abortion, war and poverty—are questions of public morality. The phrase "public morality" is at the center of the debate on religion and politics, but it is not a concept which is well understood. The degree of confusion surrounding it in this political campaign is distressing.

The problem is partially due to the collapsing of two distinct questions into one argument. One question is how—in the objective order of law and policy—we determine which issues are *public* moral questions and which are best defined as *private* moral questions. A second question is the following: How, in the face of an issue of public morality, should a public official relate personal convictions about religion and moral truths to the fulfillment of public duty? Murray offered us some essential ideas on the first question; he did not address the second.

For Murray, an issue was one of public morality if it affected the *public order* of society. Public order, in turn, encompassed three goods: public peace, essential protection of human rights, and commonly accepted standards of moral behavior in a community. Whether a given question should be interpreted as one of public morality is not always self-evident. A rationally persuasive case has to be made that an action violates the rights of others or that the consequences of actions on a given issue are so important to society that the authority of the State and the civil law ought to be invoked to govern personal and group behavior.

Obviously, in a religiously pluralistic society, getting consensus on what constitutes a public moral question is never easy. But we have been able to do it—by a process of debate, decisions, then review of our decisions.

Two cases exemplify how we have struggled with public morality in the past. First, prohibition is an example of an attempt to legislate behavior in an area ultimately decided to be beyond the reach of civil law, and not sufficiently public in nature to affect the public order. Second, civil rights, particularly in areas of housing, education, employment, voting and access to public facilities, were determined—after momentous struggles of war, politics and law—to be so central to public order that the State could not be neutral on the question.

Today, we have a public consensus in law and policy which clearly defines civil rights as issues of public morality, and the decision to drink alcoholic beverages as clearly one of private morality. Neither decision was reached without struggle. There was not an automatic public consensus on either question. Philosophers, activists, politicians, preachers, judges and ordinary citizens had to state a case, shape a consensus, and then find a way to give the consensus public standing in the life of the nation. The fact that a spontaneous public consensus is lacking at a given moment does not prohibit its being created. When he was told that the law could not legislate morality, Martin Luther King, Jr., used to say that the law could not make people love their neighbors but it could stop their lynching them. Law and policy can be instruments of shaping a public consensus; they are not simply the product of consensus.

The debate about public morality is inherent in a pluralistic society; it will never end. Today we struggle about the status of abortion. One of the valuable insights of my good and esteemed friend, Archbishop John O'Connor, articulated in his address on October 15, was that the *Roe v. Wade* decision had undercut a solid prevailing consensus against abortion on demand. The need of the moment is to reformulate a public view of the meaning of abortion.

The Catholic bishops have consistently held that abortion is without question an issue of public morality because the unborn child's right to life is at stake. Precisely because the right to life is the foundation of other rights, we see the abortion issue in the same category as civil rights questions. This is not sectarian theology, but sound public moral philosophy. The Supreme Court decision and its supporters have relegated abortion to the status of private morality—one in which society does not have an abiding interest. The entire logic of the seamless garment approach points the other way. By connecting abortion with other acknowledged human rights concerns, we seek to overcome the dangerous dichotomy which was introduced into our public life by the *Roe v. Wade* decision. We will not protect other rights securely, if we erode the right to life in our law.

The case the Catholic Bishops have made is a moral case with direct legal consequences. In his October 14th statement, Bishop James Malone, President of the National Conference of Catholic Bishops, said: "We realize that citizens and public officials may agree with our moral arguments while disagreeing with us and among themselves on the most effective legal and policy remedies . . . In debating such matters there is much room for dialogue about what constitute effective workable responses; but the debate should not be about whether a response in the political order is needed."[12]

Bishop Malone makes two central points which I want to endorse and expand upon. First, as a nation we must break through the present impasse in the abortion debate. The fact of 1.5 million abortions is a tragic reality. The very magnitude of the problem should be sufficient to establish a consensus that we have a *public problem* even if we recognize as a society that we differ about how to respond to it. As Bishop Malone said, the debate should not be *whether* a public response is needed.

Second, the distinction Bishop Malone makes between moral principle and political/legal strategies makes a significant contribution to the national debate and to the discussion within the Catholic community. On a series of questions from nuclear to social policy, the Bishops advocate both moral principles and specific solutions. In the war and peace pastoral we called specific attention to the room for debate which exists at the level of particular strategies. We need the same kind of discussion in the Church and in the country on *how* to respond to the abortion problem in the legal sphere.

As an example of the kind of open discussion we need, I would endorse the suggestion of both Archbishop O'Connor and Father Theodore Hesburgh that we initiate a national dialogue on steps to restrict the present policy of abortion on demand. To enter—indeed, to initiate—a process of restricting abortion legally is not to change Catholic teaching on the morality of abortion. It is to recognize the different roles played by moral law and civil law in a pluralistic society. The civil law must be rooted in the moral law, but it may not at times incorporate the full range of the moral law. Along with Bishop Malone, Archbishop O'Connor and all the bishops, I am committed to teaching the total moral law. But I am also committed to the search for what is possible and most effective in the civil arena.

This kind of careful distinguishing of the issues in the debate on public morality will set a better context in which to probe the second problem of personal conviction and public duty. It is an abiding problem of politics; every public figure faces the question. A few like Edmund Burke and Abraham Lincoln have put their thoughts in writing. To use a distinction I invoked earlier, the second question is not *whether* the deepest personal convictions of politicians should influence their public choices, but *how* the two should be related.

Clearly we do want people in public office whose deepest beliefs shape their character and determine the quality of their leadership. We choose public officials in part because we hope they will infuse public life with certain convictions. However, relating convictions to policy choices is a complex process. But it is precisely the complexity which should be debated.

As a theme for the debate, I find a sentence from Pope John Paul II's address to scientists and scholars at Hiroshima very suggestive. Speaking of the nuclear threat, he said: "From now on it is only through a conscious choice and through a deliberate policy that humanity can survive." This sentence spans the two dimensions of personal choice and public policy. Policy emerges as the result of conscious choices by individuals.

But the development of public policy requires a wider consensus than the personal conviction of any individual—even a public figure. Whether we look at the problem of how to reverse the arms race or how to reverse the policy of abortion on demand, the beginning of the process is a series of conscious choices that something different must be done. Then the search for deliberate policy can begin.

I would not want a candidate for public office today to be complacent, passive or satisfied with the level or the dynamic of the arms race or the defense budget of our nation. I would look for the person who says, "What we have is unacceptable, and I will work for change." The process of change will surely not be simple, but the conscious choice and the willingness to change policy are the key. In the same vein, I would want candidates who are willing to say, "The fact of 1.5 million abortions a year is unacceptable, and I will work for a change in the public policy which encourages or permits this practice." In both areas—the arms race and abortion—it will take conscious decisions by citizens and public officials if we are to have deliberate policies which serve human life.

This address has gone on too long! I plead understanding based on the complexity and centrality of the problem I was asked to address. I shall test your endurance with one final thought. The issues of religion and politics, theology and policy, public morality and personal choice will be with us long after the current election is over. Elections are wonderful and necessary events in the democratic process. However, they are not well suited for producing reflective ideas or careful distinctions. The questions which have run through this election—about the role of religion in our public life, the relation of political responses to moral issues—are broader and deeper than election politics can handle. I recommend that we use the experiences of the moment to help set the agenda for the future.

The questions of public policy raised in this election year have been formulated in the political arena. Solid answers to them will require reaching beyond politics to universities, research centers, libraries, churches and synagogues. I hope our Catholic universities will take the challenge seriously. I know the bishops will remain in the public debate, and we need help. Public officials will remain in the line of fire, and they need help. Citizens will ultimately make the difference, and they need the aid of institutions to advance the dialogue about conscious choices and deliberate policies on a range of issues.

As the debate proceeds, let us remember a favorite term of John Courtney Murray: the need for *civility*. We can keep our deepest convictions and still keep our civil courtesy. We can test others' arguments but not question their motives. We can presume good will even when we strenuously disagree. We can relate the best of religion to the best of politics in the service of each other and the wider society, national and human, to which we are bound in hope and love.

The Consistent Ethic of
Life and Public Policy

USCC Diocesan Social Action Directors' Conference
Washington, D.C.
February 10, 1988

When I was invited to give this address on "The Consistent Ethic of Life and Public Policy," my schedule for this month was already overcommitted. But I was convinced that I should not miss this opportunity, and so I simply forced the event on to my calendar. The opportunity which this topic provides has two dimensions: first, to address a crucial but still undeveloped part of the Consistent Ethic—its public application; and second, to engage with you as social action directors in a joint reflection on how the policy implications of the Consistent Ethic may be advanced.

To initiate this reflection, I will first review the origins of the concept of the Consistent Ethic, then analyze its development in the Church, and, finally, examine its public policy potential in U.S. society.

1. The Origins of the Idea

One way to explain the origins of the Consistent Ethic is to see it as an expression of the model of social teaching found in *Gaudium et spes,* the Pastoral Constitution on the Church in the Modern World of the Second Vatican Council. This conciliar document, which stands as the Magna Carta of social ministry since Vatican II, asserted that the social task of the Church in the modern world is to read the signs of the times and to interpret them in light of the gospel. The idea of the Consistent Ethic arose for me in precisely this way.

It is possible to distinguish three challenges in the contemporary signs of the times which pose different but interrelated questions for the Church's social ministry. There is the *technological* challenge, the *peace* challenge, and the *justice* challenge. The three must be interpreted in light of the gospel truth about the sacredness of human life and the obligations of Christians to stand for life.

The *technological* challenge arises from the unique capacities which contemporary science and its medical applications have produced in our generation. This challenge is most clearly visible at the beginning and the end of life. At both ends of the spectrum of life—the mystery of conception and the mystery of death—our generation has developed capacities to intervene in the natural order in ways which earlier generations would have thought belonged solely to God. Today, from genetics through embryology to the care of the aged and the terminally ill, we confront the potential of shaping the beginning of life, making choices about its development, and sustaining it by life support systems.

At both ends of the spectrum of life the technological challenge has been experienced as a blessing and a burden. Some discoveries help us to enhance life expectancy, to correct inherited genetic defects, and to relieve pain and suffering. But the new technologies have also placed in human hands decisions about life and death for which there is little human experience to guide our choices.

As Pope John Paul II has often noted, the danger of our day is that we will use our technological genius to erode human dignity rather than to enhance it. The danger is that our choices will be dominated by technology rather than directed by human wisdom and the light of faith. Precisely for this reason, the Congregation for the Doctrine of the Faith last year issued an "Instruction on Respect for Human Life in Its Origins and on the Dignity of Procreation" which addresses the moral implications of some of the biomedical techniques which now make it possible to intervene in the initial phase of the life of a human being and in the very processes of procreation.

These questions of technology, life, and death are not, however, limited to the world of science and medicine. The unique moral character of our day is demonstrated by the linkage between the "micro-questions" of medical ethics and the "macro-questions" of war and peace in the nuclear age. The link between these two quite different areas of human existence is the technologcial revolution which has unlocked the genetic code and unleashed the power of the atom within the space of a lifetime. The technological challenge is part of the *peace* challenge: how to keep the peace in an age when the instruments of war can threaten the very fabric of human existence as a whole.

Technology provides the material link between the "micro" and the "macro" threats to life in our time. The moral link is the unique value of human life. In very different settings—in the laboratory and in the life of nations—our generation is called to protect the fragile fabric of human dignity against unprecedented dangers.

Seeing the relationship—the connection—between these two areas of contemporary life is what started my reflection on the Consistent Ethic. In a special way, my chairmanship of the bishops' committee which drafted *The Challenge of Peace* and the committee presently writing the report on the moral evaluation of deterrence policy,[13] along with my chairmanship of the bishops' Pro-Life Committee, helped me to see the common challenge of technology for life and death in the two areas I have just described.

The *justice* challenge poses a different but related set of questions. It calls us to expand our moral concern beyond the question of protecting life from attack to promoting and enhancing the dignity of human life in society. The justice challenge is how to build a society which provides the necessary material and moral support for every human being to realize his or her God-given dignity. As Christians, aware of the limits of human nature and the impact of sin on human affairs, we know that this work of shaping a humane society is a never-ending task. But this sober conviction that perfect justice is a characteristic of the completed reign of God does not mean that progress toward the conditions of the Kingdom is impossible. The reign of God is present when human dignity is defended and human rights are protected. The justice challenge calls us to this effort.

In the late 1980s the justice challenge is evident on several fronts:

- twenty years after the death of Dr. Martin Luther King, Jr., there are very disturbing signs of increased racial tension in the land;
- after almost a decade of neglect our housing problem yields the tragedy of the homeless and the looming catastrophe of more homeless families; (Just last week the Holy See's Commission on Justice and Peace issued a document entitled, "What Have You Done to Your Homeless Brother? The Church and the Housing Problem," which addresses this worldwide problem.)
- on our farms and outside our factories, there is still too much evidence that a decade of economic growth and a lower rate of unemployment still has left too many vulnerable to economic devastation.

Each of these challenges—technology, peace, and justice—has its own inner complexity. Each must be addressed on its own terms by slow, patient work. No one can do everything, and I am sure that you feel closer, experientially and vocationally, to some of the issues I have described than to others.

The Consistent Ethic recognizes the need for specific approaches to concrete issues, but it also raises a broader question. Are the Church and society well served by keeping these questions in isolated sectors of life and ministry? Do we not learn something about the personal and social challenge of this moment in history by consciously connecting what is usually addressed separately?

The Consistent Ethic sees the convergence of these multiple and diverse challenges as a time of opportunity. The opportunity resides in the character of Catholic moral teaching and in the capacity of the Church to respond to multiple challenges under the guidance of a coherent moral vision.

The concept of the Consistent Ethic is based upon two characteristics of Catholic teaching: its scope and its structure. The scope of Catholic teaching is broad enough to encompass the three distinct challenges I have outlined. We are simultaneously committed to a diverse set of objectives which many individuals and institutions in U.S. society find irreconcilable. We are committed to reversing *Roe v. Wade* and reversing the arms race. We are convinced that we cannot have a just and compassionate society unless our care extends to both sides of the line of birth: We must protect the basic right to life and, at the same time, promote the associated rights of nutrition, housing, and health care which enhance the lives we have saved.

The scope of a comprehensive ethic is matched by a systematic structure of moral argument. It is not sufficient to face these three challenges of technology, peace, and justice only with good intentions. The problems posed in each area are inherently complex, and, on a number of these issues—from the Strategic Defense Initiative to health insurance to amniocentesis—U.S. society is deeply divided. A broad moral concern must be based upon solid moral analysis. A systematic moral tradition is necessary to call the ecclesial community to a position and then to project a position in the civil debate.

The Catholic moral tradition is both *simple* and *sophisticated*. It is *simple* in terms of its basic purpose: the protection and promotion of human dignity, understood as a reflection of the image of God within us. Catholic social ethics, medical ethics, and sexual ethics are all rooted in the nature and dignity of the person. This is the simple but fundamental starting point, for example, for documents as different in content as the two pastoral letters of the U.S. bishops on social ethics (war and peace, and the economy) and the Holy See's instruction last year on medical ethics (to which I referred a moment ago). Obviously, this single starting point is then developed in a highly systematic and *sophisticated* fashion so as to address in a detailed way the technological, peace, and justice challenges of our day.

The idea of the Consistent Ethic is to draw upon the scope and structure of the Catholic moral vision to confront the full range of questions endangering human dignity today. The idea must be linked to a community—a constituency—which holds and embodies the vision. A vision without a community is not capable of influence. A vision tied to a committed community is the first prerequisite of serious social impact. Hence, it is necessary now to examine how the idea of the Consistent Ethic has engaged the life of the ecclesial community.

2. The Consistent Ethic in the Church

In proposing the Consistent Ethic concept in 1983, I said that I wished to *begin* a discussion, not end one. In the four years since that first lecture on the topic, my hope for careful consideration of the idea has been realized. The concept has acted as a catalyst; it started a process. And the product of that process has been a vigorous discussion within the Catholic community about the meaning of the Consistent Ethic of Life and its potential in the Church and in civil society. The response, of course, has not meant unanimous agreement with the idea or its implications. But the process as a whole has produced a solid consensus in support of the idea, even though it is not yet a finished design in my mind or in the minds of its supporters. One may point to several levels of the life of the Church where the Consistent Ethic has had a useful impact.

First, the idea is a concept in moral theology, so the response of the theological community is very important. The attention given to explaining and refining the idea in theological journals and in a recent symposium at Loyola University in Chicago has been a crucial contribution to shaping an ecclesial consensus on the concept. As always, the doubts and reservations theologians have about an idea may be as helpful as their support, because an idea which is this far-reaching requires development.

Second, a most important step has been the explicit incorporation of the Consistent Ethic theme into the pro-life activities of the National Conference of Catholic Bishops. The use of this concept by the episcopal conference gives us a framework within which we may pursue the multifaceted agenda of the bishops at the national level.

Third, I am aware that the Consistent Ethic has been used creatively and extensively by you who labor in the Church's social ministry. The framework of the Consistent Ethic has made it possible to incorporate some of our key social themes in the Church's wider ministry. In some places it has served as a means of bridging pro-life and other social justice concerns. I am aware, here in the Washington and Baltimore Archdioceses, of the legislative network which has effectively pressed the case for the unborn, then successfully achieved a reallocation of the state budget on behalf of the poor, and also linked these concerns with national advocacy to restrain defense spending. Other such efforts at the level of dioceses, state Catholic conferences, and religious communities have demonstrated that the Consistent Ethic is an idea with a constituency.

Finally, I would like to call attention to two developments beyond the Catholic community which point to the as yet unrealized potential of the Consistent Ethic. First, an ecumenical organization *Justlife* has been formed by Catholics and Protestants to support the Consistent Ethic concept. Second, the recent Times-Mirror public attitude survey has shown a solid and intriguing pattern of a constituency which joins a liberal social justice consensus and opposition to liberalized abortion.

Both the ecumenical initiative and the secular trend create a context within which the Consistent Ethic can provide a viable social agenda. This is a potential yet to be realized; it is hardly a sure thing. But all these developments inside and outside the Church point to my final point: the public policy potential of the Consistent Ethic.

3. The Idea, the Community, and Public Policy

It is useful to note from the beginning of this discussion that a primary purpose of the Consistent Ethic theme has been to increase the Church's public policy effectiveness in the United States. The Consistent Ethic provides a framework within which a range of policy issues may be pursued in a coordinated fashion. It also provides a method for establishing priorities among these many issues. Finally, it provides a method for resolving conflicts at the tactical level when some issues are in conflict.

The Consistent Ethic's public policy focus expresses the strong social orientation of all Catholic moral theology. It is not the position of this tradition that all moral values and principles should be legislated. But every stream of moral thinking which feeds into the Consistent Ethic— social ethics, medical ethics, sexual ethics—is based on the conviction that some key values, principles, and practices must be protected and promoted by law and public policy.

That is why we believe it is inadequate merely to teach that cultural, sexual, and racial discrimination are wrong; it is also necessary to outlaw discrimination in civil law. We are morally convinced that a just wage is needed to protect human dignity; but we also know that minimum wage laws are absolutely necessary. We are convinced that protection for unborn children cannot rely only upon moral persuasion; their lives must be protected, as our lives are, by the civil law.

These issues I have just cited as examples are among the priority items on the episcopal conference's legislative agenda. To fill out the Consistent Ethic would require a detailed listing of issues, but I do not think that would be the best use of our time this evening.

It is wiser, I believe, to highlight the several roles which the Consistent Ethic can play in public advocacy. First, it may and should be used nationally and locally. Particularly in this meeting, the national and local possibilities are clear. You are being briefed on the USCC national legislative agenda which is set in terms of the Consistent Ethic. But the same framework may be given different content at the local or diocesan level. The Consistent Ethic is not a rigid set of specific issues. It is a method for coordinating a spectrum of issues; and there are local issues which belong in the Consistent Ethic.

Second, the Consistent Ethic provides a grid for assessing party platforms and the records of candidates for public office. It is a broad-based set of criteria. Properly used, the Consistent Ethic will refute decisively claims that we are a "one-issue" constituency. The essence of the Consistent Ethic argument is that no one issue can exhaust the moral significance of our public policy concerns.

Third, the Consistent Ethic provides the scope of moral vision which allows the Church to address broad policy issues embodying several distinct moral concerns. Perhaps the best example is the Federal Budget. The Budget, in a very real sense, is a moral document; it puts a price tag on what we value as a nation. The Budget is also, of course, a complex technical document which is at the center of our national life.

The battle over the budget, a perennially important political question, has taken on new moral intensity in a time of persistent deficits. The deficits impose a straitjacket on the budget process: to vote funds in one place is to take them away from other concerns. There is little spare change in the U.S. Treasury to adjudicate the conflict in the policy process.

Faced with this policy problem, the Consistent Ethic provides a framework for addressing the central budgetary trade-off—defense spending vs. social spending—and it also provides a basis for lifting up specific issues with high moral content.

A good example, in my judgment, of the kind of issues which may be effectively highlighted by the Consistent Ethic is the needs of children. In the last four years a series of studies have demonstrated that the most fragile members of our society, children, are also the least protected. From infant mortality statistics—which place us near the bottom of industrialized countries—to health care, to housing—children's lives are under assault in our culture.

A century ago Dostoyevsky said that the death of an innocent child was enough to destroy belief in God. Less dramatically, the suffering of innocent children is enough to indict the social priorities of a wealthy society. There is a consensus developing from the business community, to politicians, to child advocacy groups that a major coordinated effort on behalf of children is both a moral imperative and a national political necessity. Spending on children is cost-effective in the long run. But it requires wisdom and courage to mount the effort to spend now—even with deficits—on this solid investment in our nation's future.

The Consistent Ethic is anchored in a concern for unborn children; it is shaped in terms of the strong Catholic commitment to the family; and it is directed toward a preferential concern for the poor. All of these themes may be placed in support of a coherent, coordinated strategy to enhance the life of children from conception through high school graduation.

This example has a moral priority and a strong political potential, but it is only part of the larger vision we are invited to pursue through the Consistent Ethic. I am committed to this moral vision and committed to building a constituency for it. Your positions in dioceses across the country make you uniquely valuable allies. I pledge my support to your work and, along with my fellow bishops, I know we can count on the continuing high quality and deep dedication of your work. Together, we have an opportunity to share the reality of the Consistent Ethic with the society we are called to serve.

Euthanasia:
Ethical and Legal Challenge

The Center for Clinical Medical Ethics
University of Chicago Hospital
May 26, 1988

It is a pleasure for me to return to the University of Chicago and, in particular, to this prestigious medical center. I am very grateful to the Center for Clinical Medical Ethics for inviting me to give this address. Dr. Mark Siegler contacted me at a time when I was already deeply concerned about recent efforts to legalize euthanasia. I have been eager to participate more actively in the public discussion about this new challenge in our society.

Since I accepted his invitation, the issue has become even more pressing, especially in the debate that has followed the publication of the article, "It's Over, Debbie," in the *Journal of the American Medical Association*.[14] And so, I assure you that I look forward to the responses and the discussion which will follow my presentation, as well as the colloquium later this afternoon.

My reflections will have four parts. First, I will explore the pluralistic context of the discussion of the public policy dimensions of euthanasia. Second, I will trace some of the reasons why euthanasia or assisted suicide has become a matter of current debate. Third, I will outline a moral or ethical perspective on euthanasia. And fourth, I will suggest how we might best respond to this challenge.

1. Euthanasia: A Matter of Public Policy

One of the hallmarks of our democratic system of government and our social environment here in the United States is the fact that a plurality of views informs our public discourse regarding fundamental human questions. At times, these views flow from religious beliefs. At other times, they derive from philosophical or pragmatic judgments about the meaning and purpose of life.

59

This pluralism is the result of the free speech accorded by the Constitution to each citizen as well as the right both to freely exercise one's religion and to practice *no* religion. But this constitutionally protected pluralism has not been bought at the price of excluding religious or moral values from the public life of the nation. On the contrary, the goal of the American system has been to provide space for a moral or religious substance in our society.

Indeed, in our pluralistic society we must decide how those who have such beliefs or ethical principles may appropriately participate in the development of public policy. In my view, positions that are informed by particular religious beliefs or philosophical assumptions need to be translated into commonly agreed upon language, arguments, and categories before they can become the moral or ethical foundations for key public policy choices.

I am speaking here of *public* policy decisions. Because of the nature of our government and our social order, we have determined that certain areas of human life—although they have important ethical or moral dimensions—are not immediately or necessarily appropriate subject matter for public policies. Although the premises or foundations for public policy and civil law ought to be rooted in an ethical perspective, the scope of law and public policy is limited, and its purpose is not the moralization of society. Public policy decisions and civil statutes address primarily external acts and values that affect the common good.

But how do we determine which aspects of our life—whether social or personal—are subject to public policy decisions? A leading Catholic theoretician in this area, the late Father John Courtney Murray, argued that an issue was related to public policy if it affected the public order of society. And public order, in turn, encompassed three goods: public peace, the essential protection of human rights, and commonly accepted standards of moral behavior in a community.

Whether a given issue should be interpreted as belonging to public morality is not always self-evident. A rationally persuasive case must be made that an action violates the rights of another or that the consequences of actions on a given issue are so important to society that the authority of the State ought to be invoked, through public policy or civil statute, to govern personal and group behavior. Obviously, in a pluralistic society, arriving at a consensus on what pertains to public policy is never easy. But we have been able to achieve such consensus in the past by a process of dialogue, decision-making, and review of our decisions.

Our nation has developed its public policy and civil law through dialogue—first of all, about what aspects of human behavior ought to be regulated by public policy decisions and, then, about which ethical or moral perspective should guide the development of such policies. As a society, our constitutional structure and our historical experience indicate that it is appropriate for persons with a religiously or philosphically informed perspective to participate in these discussions. Moreover, we have learned that the best way to facilitate this participation is by translating religious or philosophical views into a common language that can guide and inform public policy decisions.

In regard to euthanasia or assisted suicide, the kind of decision-making which I have just described has already taken place. Long ago our predecessors determined that the taking of innocent life was contrary to the public good—even if it is done to alleviate pain or suffering. And consequently, it has been judged as being in the best interest of society to stop a person who is trying to jump from a bridge, and to impose civil penalties on those who engage in euthanasia or assist a person in suicide.

This public policy decision, informed by an ethical or moral understanding of the nature and meaning of human life, is being challenged today on two fronts. First, does the state have any interest in this matter, or should it be left up to the individual? Second, is euthanasia truly contrary to the public good?

2. Why the Movement to Legalize Euthanasia?

I now wish to turn to my second area of concern: Why is there a movement today to change our public policy on this matter? In addressing this question, we are not merely dealing with the case of "Debbie" and her doctor. There is a growing debate in our land about euthanasia and assisted suicide. There has been, for example, a special television report about the case of a Florida husband who killed his wife who had Alzheimer's Disease.

Moreover, there was the California initiative that sought not only to reaffirm the right to withdraw life-sustaining procedures but also to secure the right to provide "aid in dying" through any medical procedure that would terminate life "swiftly, painlessly, and humanely." While the sponsors lacked more than 100,000 signatures to get this issue on the November ballot, they attribute this to a lack of time to organize the drive rather than the opposition of citizens. And they have indicated they will try again.

But why are we hearing this call to alter what has been a fundamental tenet of our society? We may identify three sources, among others, for this advocacy of change. While these three sources or movements may not afford a total explanation for this phenomenon, they provide a way to begin to analyze it.

(a) Medical

The first movement flows from the world of medicine and medical technology. For centuries, the physician and others in the health care professions have had, as an essential aspect of their identity and mission, the responsibility to heal and preserve life. That responsibility has entered a new era with the development of medicines and technologies that have given physicians previously unknown capabilities in this area. We are grateful, indeed, for the great good which these advancements have brought to the human family.

This good, however, has not been an unmixed blessing. We know that it is fairly easy for technology or medicine to become an end in itself, and for life to be preserved when, in fact, death should be allowed to happen. This possible domination of technology over the proper course of life has left many people fearful of being kept alive in an inhumane fashion. And this fear has led some to say to their loved ones: "Do whatever you must, but do not let me live that way." The fear, then, of the pain and discomfort of a life prolonged inappropriately has led to an erosion of the natural instinct to preserve one's own life.

(b) Legal

The second cause of the movement towards euthanasia involves two aspects of the legal dimension of our society. First, we have become a "contentious" society. The right to redress a wrong done to a person by another is now being actualized as it has never been before in our society. As you know, the medical profession and the health care industry have experienced countless lawsuits and settlements that make them fearful of future damages.

The result has been that, in certain critical decisions involving living and dying, many perceive that the focus of concern may no longer be the good of the patient—as that has been traditionally understood by our Judeo-Christian moral tradition. Instead, the concern will be whatever will best protect the physician and the health care institution from legal action. Many point out that decisions, which formerly have been made by the physician and the patient or the patient's family, are now made by legal counsel or the court.

What has been the result? Not only have people come to fear technology, they also fear losing a fundamental right—the right to self-determination. The combination of these two fears—the fear of the inappropriate use of medical technology and the loss of self-determination—have joined another movement in our society: the expanding notion of the right of privacy.

There is not time in this presentation to elaborate upon what Robert Bellah and others have said recently—that we have lost a sense of community in our society and witnessed the rise of an exaggerated concept of individualism. My pastoral experience confirms that there is some truth in their observations. Translated into the world of law, this separation of the individual from a community context has been expressed in a growing number of legal decisions that have expanded the notion of the right to privacy to such an issue as the taking of pre-natal life.

It is but a next logical step to conclude that the individual should be autonomous in determining matters pertaining to the *end* of life. In our contemporary society an exaggerated *individualism* replaces concern and responsibility for the *common good*. This, in turn, becomes a welcome environment to discuss the fear of technology and the loss of self-determination. And in the light of this momentum, it is understandable that persons who ask family or friends to keep them from an unseemly death would think that those fulfilling this wish should not be prosecuted for doing a "good deed."

(c) Cultural

With this consideration of the rise of individualism, and its legal expression, we come face to face with the third movement—our culture itself. Again, I will only be able to use broad strokes to describe a complex phenomenon under three headings: our culture's fixation on youth, our loss of meaning and consequent fear of suffering and death, and our experience of diminishing resources.

It is no secret that our society has become fairly fixated on youth and health. We seek to delay the effects of aging, and the pursuit of being healthy has become a significant growth industry. It is striking that this is occurring when more and more of our citizens are becoming older and their health more fragile. This contrast between our idealized notions and real life can have two effects. Those who are older and not so healthy may question whether they ought to continue living. And those who are younger and supposedly healthy may reject those who remind them of their own human frailty.

Likewise, our society is raising profound questions about the ultimate meaning of life. While it had once been assumed that pain and sacrifice were part of the human experience and contributed to the meaning of life, many would question that assumption today. An ethos of instant gratification does not suffer pain or sacrifice easily. A world whose meaning is centered in a seemingly unlimited present moment may interpret death as a purely human event, devoid of any relationship to a divinity who sustains a truly endless eternity.

Finally, living in the shadow of the earlier oil embargo and the more recent Space Shuttle disaster, our society has come face to face with the constraints of physical and intellectual resources. The American myth of the ever-expanding horizon which can be conquered by determination and skill has been shattered. Wherever we turn, we are faced with hard choices about the allocation of resources and the setting of individual and national priorities.

These three aspects of our culture, and others, are the context of the current discussion of euthanasia. A culture that does not prize the wisdom of aging and feels intimidated by ill health will be less likely to oppose the ending of an aged or infirm life. A culture that is devoid of a vision of values that transcend time and individual choice will be more likely to feel no discomfort with an immediate solution. And a culture of youth and immediacy will be uncomfortable with the allocation of precious fiscal and health resources to those who are marginal or sick.

When this third movement encounters the first two, then we should not be surprised by the fact that some are calling for a change in our public policy—a change that would legalize euthanasia. But does this mean we must accept what is being proposed?

3. Why Oppose Euthanasia?

This leads me to my third subject: an ethical or moral perspective that can serve as the foundation for public policy development. I will discuss two issues here: the argument against euthanasia, and why this should be a matter for public policy.

The foundation of my position on euthanasia is to be found in what I have described as a Consistent Ethic of Life. As you may know, over the last four and a half years I have articulated the need for a Consistent Ethic of Life. I have proposed it as a comprehensive concept and a strategy which will help Catholics and other people of good will to influence more effectively the development of public policy in our nation.

The grounding principle for this ethic is found in the Judeo-Christian heritage which has played such an influential role in the formation of our national ethos. In this religious tradition, the meaning of human life is grounded in the fact that it is sacred because God is its origin and its destiny. Many other people of good will also accept the basic premise that human life has a distinctive dignity and meaning or purpose, and that innocent human life must not be directly attacked, threatened, or diminished. They, too, argue that, because of the privileged meaning of human life, we are responsible to steward, protect, and nurture it.

The second principle which informs the development of the Consistent Ethic is the belief that human life is also social in nature. We do not come into being to live alone, but to move from the dependency of pre-natal existence and infancy to the interrelatedness of adulthood. To be human is to be social, and those relationships, structures, and institutions which support us as individuals and as a community are an essential aspect of human life.

If one accepts these two principles about human life, then one may argue that two precepts or obligations necessarily flow from them. The first is that, as individuals and as a society, we have the *positive* obligation to protect life. The second precept is that we have the *negative* obligation not to destroy or injure human life directly, especially the life of the innocent and vulnerable.

This perspective about life and the precepts just mentioned were, in effect, recognized by and incorporated into our Anglo-Saxon common law tradition. Consequently, it has been reasoned that the protection of innocent life—and, therefore, opposition to abortion, murder, suicide, and euthanasia—pertains to the common good of society. As social beings, we cannot violate one of the constitutive goods of life. Consequently, our legal tradition has developed statutes that outlaw murder and euthanasia. In other words, our tradition has held that euthanasia is wrong because it involves a direct attack on innocent human life. And it is a matter of public policy because it involves a violation of a fundamental human good.

Having laid out the principles, let us turn now to the arguments being advanced against this traditional perspective.

The first argument attacks the premise that the obligation to protect and nurture human life applies to life that is painful and unable to achieve its full human potential. Although I will elaborate on this in the last section of my presentation, I wish to mention here that our first response to this line of reasoning must be—to use an analogy from the teaching of grammar—to parse the question and make clear what we are saying when we uphold the obligation to protect and nurture human life, even when it is painful or dying.

We are saying that those whose lives have, in fact, entered the dying process should be helped to live the remainder of their lives with full human dignity and with as little pain as possible. We also are saying that those measures which we would consider to be ethically extraordinary need not be used to prolong life. We also are saying that, when considered on a case by case basis and in light of our ethical principles, there are situations when we can withdraw what have become useless or burdensome measures.

In this nuanced context, we are opposed to creating *a priori* categories of persons whose lives no longer need be protected, where life is no longer seen as being sacred and inviolable. Once we begin saying that a certain category of persons or a specific individual—for whatever reason, and whether the person is conscious or unconscious—no longer possesses human dignity, then we have assumed a prerogative which belongs only to God. Human rights may then be given or withdrawn as arbitrarily as they were in the Third Reich of yesterday or in South Africa today. The dignity of innocent life is absolute; it cannot be violated.

The second argument pertains to the development of public policy. Some argue that one may hold to this line of moral reasoning, but that the actual determination of how to end life should be left to the individual involved. The State has no interest in what is essentially a private decision.

As I indicated earlier, the perspective which supports this line of reasoning is fundamentally flawed. Human beings are meant to live in community. Social order is not an enemy but a necessary good that protects personal and social life. Kept in proper balance, the tension between personal rights and social goods can be healthy. And nowhere is this more evident than in matters pertaining to the defense and enhancement of life itself. Neither individuals nor society can long survive when respect for the inviolability of life is diminished. It is for this reason that the protection of innocent life must be understood as part of the public order of society. As such, it legitimately fits within the scope of civil law. The state has a moral and legal interest in protecting innocent life from conception to natural death.

We live in an age when violence has become part of our national fabric. We bury young people killed in gang violence. We read about persons who kill others in a dispute about which television program to watch. Is this *good* for us as individuals or as a society? No!

What would we be suggesting to one another and to our society, if, seemingly with the best of motives, we were to say that those who are sick, infirm, or unconscious may be killed? How could we allege that such actions would not affect us individually and collectively? We may never agree to this kind of privatization of life because, if we were to do so, we would undermine our ability to live in community. Life is both a private and a public good, and, therefore, social legislation to defend and protect it is both appropriate and necessary.

4. What Are We to Do Next?

Having argued against euthanasia and attempts to legalize it, what are we to do next?

We cannot pretend that "It's Over, Debbie" and the California initiative have not happened. Like it or not, the issue of euthanasia has become a question that will be answered, among other places, in the oncology wards and the legislatures of our land. And it will not be enough for those who oppose this movement merely to speak out against it. We should not yield the "high ground" of the language of compassion and personal rights to those whose views we oppose. On the contrary, in a manner faithful to our pluralistic heritage, we must engage this challenge forthrightly and persuasively. I would like to propose some of the ways in which we might do this.

First, it is important for us to address the sense of powerlessness which many people experience in regard to the contemporary practice of medicine. While the catchphrase "patient as person" is a helpful guide in this matter, we have to extend this concept more aggressively into the world of critical and terminal illness where the patient is frailest and most vulnerable. We must also face our own fear of death and learn to provide for those who are dying or critically ill in a way that preserves their dignity and ennobles them.

For example, in light of available medicines, is it conscionable that a dying patient should unwillingly suffer great pain today? I think not. Moreover, is it necessary for so many patients to die on a machine? Resolving such questions may require finding ways to provide the necessary funding, through the allocation of insurance and public monies, to establish and maintain hospice units in hospitals as well as to provide hospice programs in patients' homes. In this way we can eliminate many of the legitimate concerns that may motivate people to consider euthanasia— which otherwise would be unacceptable to them and society.

Second, we must face in a forthright manner the ethical and legal issues pertaining to the initiation and/or cessation of medical procedures that are ethically "extraordinary," and thus not morally obligatory. I refer to those procedures that have no reasonable hope of success, that are not likely to produce significant benefit for the patient, and that the Catholic tradition considers to be extremely burdensome, that is, extremely painful and costly. As citizens and leaders in our society, we must engage our legislatures and judicial system in a dialogue to find ways to ensure that appropriate medical decisions are made by patients or their surrogates, in consultation with the physician and others. If this process is improved, fewer physicians and health care institutions may feel a need to refer these decisions to the courts out of fear of legal liability.

Third, the controverted question of the artificial provision of nutrition and hydration for several categories of patients needs to be resolved. We cannot accept a policy that would open the door to euthanasia by creating categories of patients whose lives can be considered of no value merely because they are not conscious. We also may not develop a policy to keep alive those who should be allowed a natural death, that is, those who are terminally ill, or to preclude a decision—informed by our ethical principles and on a case by case basis—that the artificial provision of nutrition and hydration has become useless or unduly burdensome.

I know that this is a very complex issue. I am convinced that, from a moral point of view, the essential bond between food, water, and life argues convincingly for the presumption that nutrition and hydration should always be provided. But I am also convinced that we are not *morally* obliged to do everything that is *technically* possible. In other words, there are cases where we would not be obliged artificially to provide nutrition and hydration. The challenge is to develop a nuanced public policy to protect against an attitude that could erode respect for the inviolable dignity of human life. If we do not resolve this critical issue in a way that resonates with the common sense of people of good will, then we may contribute to the sense of desperation that will lead people to consider euthanasia as an alternative solution to the problem.

Fourth, we will have to assess the current allocation of medical resources. Significant funds are spent on the care of the elderly and the critically ill. At the same time our nation, especially in certain communities like Chicago, has a poor track record in prenatal care and infant mortality. Similarly, many people in our society do not have access to needed health care, whether it be curative or preventive, because they cannot afford health insurance.

In light of these facts, it is understandable that some argue that we should rearrange our health care priorities and reduce the amount of money spent on the elderly and certain categories of illness. Before we engage in a national debate on such a proposal, however, we must ask a prior question. Are we, in fact, spending too *much* on the elderly, or are we spending too *little* on all health care?

To say it another way, are we spending too much of our financial resources on certain patients, or are our overall allocations for health care too limited? In attempting to answer these questions, we encounter a more basic set of questions—our national priorities. I mention this, not to confuse the discussion about euthanasia, but to point out that the legalization of euthanasia is not the proper way to solve the problem of inadequate care for the poor and the unborn.

Fifth, as a society we will have to address the complex issue of the separation of the individual from the community. Religious leaders must initiate a dialogue with philosophers, anthropologists, and legal scholars to discern how we can preserve the rights of the individual without eroding or destroying our social nature. We need to find a new balance between these two dimensions of human life—a balance suitable to a society in which the population is more educated and mobile, but also more afraid and isolated.

Similarly, we will not successfully oppose the legalization of euthanasia if we cannot call forth from the depths of our national psyche those values which are constitutive of the American Dream. The interaction of our political heritage and our religious traditions can provide a response to the contemporary search for meaning—a response that will recognize the wisdom of the elderly and provide a broader perspective for the problem of pain and suffering.

Sixth, and finally, we must mobilize a common effort. In dialogues such as this, we need to confront the issue directly and help form a national consensus in favor of the presumption that the State has a compelling interest in opposing euthanasia. The basis for such a consensus is already present in our land. It is our task to bring it to the fore so that it truly can be said that, as citizens, we are entitled to life and need not fear that innocent life will ever be taken.

Ethical and Policy
Issues of Deterrence

Spring 1989 Conference
State University of New York at Buffalo
May 5, 1989

At the outset, I wish to express my appreciation for the invitation to give the keynote address on the topic of "Ethical and Policy Issues of Deterrence." When the U.S. Catholic bishops were preparing their pastoral letter, *The Challenge of Peace,* in 1983, and when we returned to the topic in our *Report on the Challenge of Peace* in 1988, our primary purpose was to encourage other institutions and individuals in the United States to engage the nuclear reality in its many dimensions: political, strategic, scientific, and moral. This symposium is precisely the kind of scholarly examination which we hoped would occur. I am pleased to be part of the effort.

I realize that you have gathered here a broad array of experts from a variety of fields. This guarantees that the several interlocking pieces of the deterrence problem will be examined in detail. Because I am confident that such a detailed assessment will occur in other presentations, I have designed this keynote address so that it may serve as a broad framework for evaluating the *ethical and policy* issues of deterrence as we face the last decade of the twentieth century.

This century is destined to be known in history as the "nuclear age." In the face of all the wonderful and tragic events which have shaped the period from 1900 to 2000, the nuclear challenge will be a defining characteristic of this century. In his magisterial study of the history of the nuclear age, McGeorge Bundy has called this challenge the ongoing epic of "Danger and Survival." During the fifty years which Bundy traces, public attention to the nuclear question has followed a cyclical pattern. There have been periods of intense public concern and anxiety (reflected in literature and films as well as in politics), and there have been periods when, in columnist George Will's words, we have treated the nuclear danger with as much familiarity as the wallpaper in our homes.

The 1980s have been a decade of both public concern and policy changes in the nuclear story. Public concern has especially cut across the United States and Western Europe; and policy changes—at least in their initial steps—have engaged both the Soviet Union and the United States.

This evening, I will look *back* at the 1980s and *ahead* to the 1990s. First, I wish to comment on the significance of the nuclear debate in the past decade. Second, I will look specifically at the impact of the 1980s debate on the strategy of deterrence. Third, I will sketch characteristics of the nuclear argument which, I believe, will be prominent in the 1990s.

I. The 1980s: The Public and the Policy Argument

The 1960s were a decade of focused concern about nuclear weapons, ranging from the public fright of the Cuban Missile Crisis, to the policy achievements of the Limited Test Ban Treaty (1963) and the Nonproliferation Treaty (1968), to the intellectual breakthroughs in security and arms control studies. The 1970s were absorbed in other issues. The debate about the politics and ethics of war and peace was concentrated on Vietnam. And the intellectual and political emphasis of the 1970s was the interdependence agenda of economic issues and human rights.

But the 1980s witnessed the renewal of the nuclear argument at a new level of public sophistication. The reawakening of public concern with nuclear danger in the early 1980s, the reinvigoration of academic interest in nuclear politics, and the results of both in strategic policy and arms control are a complex story to tell.

Rather than try to sort out the competing explanations of why the pendulum of intellectual and political interest swung back to nuclear issues, I will comment on three characteristics of the 1980s debate: its *public* dimensions, its *moral* quality, and its *policy* results.

The first distinguishing mark of the 1980s nuclear discussion in the United States was its popular or *public quality*. While spurts of public interest or panic had marked the 1950s and 1960s, the broad-based, sustained, and sophisticated popular engagement in the nuclear debate over the last nine years sets this period apart from earlier years. I use "popular" here to include not only the general public, but specific professional groups which do not work primarily or directly on strategic policy.

Using this definition, one can point to the Freeze Movement of the 1980s as a truly citizen-based lobby pressing for more intensive efforts to control the nuclear competition. Joined to it was the authentically new kind of interest shown by the physicians in the 1980s. Both the Physicians for Social Responsibility in the United States and the U.S.–Soviet alliance of physicians joined under the umbrella of the International Physicians For The Prevention of Nuclear War brought a special authority and concreteness to the nuclear debate by their emphasis on the medical consequences of a nuclear exchange.

Similarly, the engagement of the religious community shaped the daunting technical nuclear discussion in a moral direction which stressed the human costs of the nuclear competition and the human responsibility to bring it under greater control. This was not a new engagement, but a renewal of early efforts now marked by greater lay interest and more specific technical understanding.

The visibility and centrality of the *moral* argument in the public policy debate was the second distinguishing characteristic of the 1980s. While the moral analysis of the threat posed by nuclear weapons had been pursued in academic and ecclesial circles since the 1950s, there had been little impact on the public debate and surprisingly little interchange between the moralists and the development of strategic studies which had marked the late 1950s and early 1960s. Both of these aspects changed in the 1980s.

On the one hand, the unique moral problems posed by the use of nuclear weapons and the strategy of deterrence came under scrutiny at the popular and policy levels of the nuclear argument in the 1980s. The Catholic pastoral letter, *The Challenge of Peace,* is often cited as the symbol and catalyst for this moral concern, but I must stress that this letter was part of a wider range of moral scrutiny of nuclear policy.

In the pre-nuclear age, the moral issues of war and peace arose when a war began. It was then that people raised the moral questions of what *purpose* justified the use of force and what *means* were permissible in warfare. Nuclear weapons, because of their new dimensions of destructiveness, raise the old question with new intensity and complexity. The moral evaluation of war has always held that the only legitimate use of force must be a limited one. The cumulative results of strategic and scientific studies about the likely consequences of escalation in a nuclear conflict have convinced many that the notion of a limited nuclear conflict is an exceedingly unlikely and dubious notion.

In addition to casting the old moral questions in a new light, the nuclear age raised a new set of moral questions. Precisely because of the strategy of deterrence—a strategy based on the threat of unleashing virtually uncontrolled nuclear force in response to a nuclear attack—the moral questions of war invaded peacetime. The new questions were not about nuclear *war* but about nuclear *peace.* Does the strategy of deterrence—the way we keep the nuclear peace—pass the moral test of right intention? Does it meet the requirements of being prepared to use only that amount of force which will be both proportionate and discriminate in its consequences? These questions posed new tests for the morality of war and peace. And the responses varied.

Some have been convinced that nuclear strategy fails both the test of *use* in warfare and that of being a morally legitimate *deterrent*. Others have expended great energy seeking to devise and define ways in which both deterrence and possible use of nuclear weapons would be morally legitimate. Still others have concluded that use would clearly be a moral failure, but deterrence—in a paradoxical way—should be maintained and justified as the only possible means known thus far to keep the nuclear peace.

In the first twenty-five years of the nuclear age, these considerations of the morality of nuclear strategy were carried on by theologians, philosophers, and lawyers. In the last decade, the renewed nuclear argument has included in the moral debate many of the political and strategic analysts of nuclear policy. The divorce of moral argument and strategic assessment has been bridged in a fashion which places the moral questions much closer to the political and strategic judgments. It would be too much to say that moral considerations control strategic judgments today, or even to say that a consensus about moral judgments exists on nuclear issues. But the shape and structure of the nuclear argument look different at the end of the 1980s than they did at the end of the 1960s or 1970s. The moral claims are in the public debate, testing it and being tested by it.

A third question which can be asked about the 1980s, beyond the public and moral aspects of the nuclear debate, is what occurred in the *public policy* arena. The decade manifested broad shifts in policy orientation. The Reagan Administration came into office convinced that efforts to control the arms race through negotiated arguments had yielded few positive results. Hence, it criticized both the SALT II Treaty and the entire style of arms control negotiations.

Moreover, the early 1980s were marked by intense superpower competition and ideological hostility. In addition, President Reagan was sufficiently convinced of the misdirection of the controlling strategy of the nuclear age that he launched a major effort to redirect it through development and deployment of the Strategic Defense Initiative. These characteristics marked the first term of the Reagan presidency.

In Mr. Reagan's second term, with Mr. Gorbachev installed as the new Soviet leader, we saw a return to arms control. Indeed, at Reykjavik the two leaders seemed eager to jump over arms control to disarmament as they discussed the possible elimination of ballistic missiles and/or all nuclear weapons.

But SDI and the inherent complexity of the nuclear balance curbed the momentary debate about zero nuclear weapons. The post-Reykjavik period of Mr. Reagan's term produced a ratified Intermediate-range Nuclear Forces Treaty (INF) and an intellectual consensus about how to move toward a deep cuts regime in renewed Strategic Arms Reduction Talks (START) negotiations. Beyond INF, the 1980s also recorded Mr. Gorbachev's withdrawal of 500,000 troops and 10,000 tanks from Eastern Europe, along with a flood of proposals about every major topic on the arms control agenda.

A decade that began with superpower hostility ended with the promise of normalization of relations. A decade which started with no arms control produced a modest agreement and the basis of a significant treaty. And a decade bedeviled by SDI is ending with the Congress and the executive branch both scaling back its scope and significance.

I do not intend this summary to communicate that control of the nuclear dilemma is a sure thing in the 1990s. We are far from anything of the kind. I only wish to point out the significance of the 1980s in terms of public engagement, moral analysis, and policy developments on the nuclear front.

II. The 1980s: Deterrence in Doubt But Not in Decline

None of these developments displaced deterrence from its central role in the superpower relationship. Yet, it is also the case that the debates of the 1980s, among both the strategists and the moralists, have had their effect on the status of deterrence.

To grasp the impact of the debates of the 1980s, it is useful to remind ourselves of how central the concept of deterrence has been to the nuclear age. Certainly since the 1950s, the idea of deterrence has been the defining concept of strategic thought. The strategic debates have been intense and prolonged, but they have been about *how much* is needed to deter and *what kind* of declaratory policy, force structure and targeting doctrine is required for credible deterrence. The strategic debate has *not* been about the wisdom of deterrence, only about its operational character.

In both strategy and ethics, the 1980s nuclear argument probed deeper than the standard strategic debates to ask the question whether deterrence is the only or the best way to deal with a world of sovereign states and nuclear arsenals. To some degree, the inquiry—both strategic and ethical—testified to the staying power of deterrence. The concept and the reality are not easily replaced, but it is instructive to review the attempts to do so.

Among moral analysts, nuclear deterrence has never found enthusiastic supporters. The notion of a "necessary evil" perhaps best conveys the judgment rendered by political and moral philosophers. Michael Walzer's intricate, almost tortured assessment of deterrence in *Just and Unjust Wars* fits this sense of deterrence as a "necessary evil" or a "lesser evil" than other alternatives.

In addition to the lack of enthusiasm among supporters of deterrence, one must add that, from the early stages of the nuclear debate, a minority of moralists have argued consistently that deterrence is evil, pure and simple. This perspective is represented by British moralists from Walter Stein in the 1960s through Anthony Kenny and John Finnis today, and is reflected here in the United States in the writings of both moral philosophers and theologians. Essentially, this perspective is not persuaded that the physical and political evils prevented by deterrence make it a moral strategy, because these moralists are convinced that the means of deterrence inevitably involve the will to threaten and, if necessary, to kill civilian populations.

In the moral argument about deterrence prior to the 1980s, the spectrum of opinion tended to run from deterrence being marginally justifiable to its not passing moral muster. What is striking about the nuclear debate of the 1980s is the way deterrence came under review and criticism in the mainline arguments of the strategic community. I use the term "review" to indicate that the concept and strategy of deterrence came under criticism, but were not discarded or displaced. Nonetheless, the criticism of deterrence in the 1980s was intellectually and politically important in the strategic debate, because it was such a shift from the tone and themes of strategic arguments in the previous two decades.

Some in the 1980s, like Michael McGwire, a scholar of Soviet affairs at the Brookings Institute, argued that "deterrence is the problem." Others, like Professor Alexander George at Stanford, made the more narrow point that deterrence is too restricted a notion to capture the dynamics and meaning of U.S.–Soviet competition. While not displaced, the vulnerabilities and limits of deterrence theory and strategy were stressed in the last decade. The results of this empirical testing involve a certain erosion of confidence that deterrence is a long-term answer to the nuclear question in world politics.

The erosion of confidence does not lead to any radical departures by the strategic theorists. Indeed, some, like Robert Tucker of Johns Hopkins, regard it as illusory and dangerous to think of deterrence as anything but a quasi-permanent part of our destiny. Deterrence, he says, "will remain a part of our 'condition' for as far as we can presently see." Tucker's view certainly reflects the strategic consensus prior to the 1980s, but the critique of the eighties has also yielded Professor Joseph Nye's view that "it is important to reduce reliance on nuclear deterrence in the long term." Nye's view stresses the stability which deterrence has manifested over four decades, but he is also willing to acknowledge the forces and factors—from technology to public psychology—which make it a shortsighted policy simply to project a future of deterrence without end. Deterrence should be a means to an end. As Nye put it recently, "We need to look at processes of influence, accommodation, and cooperation that can reduce the acuteness of the security dilemma."

This brief commentary on the changing shape of the strategic and moral assessment of deterrence in the 1980s puts in perspective the position of the U.S. Catholic bishops' two documents, *The Challenge of Peace* in 1983 and the *Report on the Challenge of Peace* in 1988. In both documents, our objective was to assess the moral status of deterrence policy in light of the role it has played in world politics over the last forty years. Our judgment of 1983 was to give *conditional* moral acceptance to deterrence. The moral judgment is designed to acknowledge that the strategy of deterrence plays a useful—indeed, necessary—role in the present international system. But the risk of failure of deterrence, the impetus the strategy provides for ongoing nuclear competition, and the resources it consumes all place a moral mortgage on deterrence. Hence, we placed conditions on our acceptance.

Conditional acceptance means, as we said in 1983, that deterrence is not a long-term answer to the nuclear dilemma. Deterrence provides space and time to search for a different political structure for the superpower relationship. The bishops' judgment of conditional acceptance of deterrence places them solidly on the side of those strategic commentators who stress the limits of deterrence as a strategy and seek to press beyond deterrence to redefining the political context of international relations.

III. The 1990s: The Primacy of the Political

Indeed, I believe the connection between the nuclear debate of the 1980s, which I have been reviewing this evening, and the nuclear question of the 1990s will be the *political* issues, not the strategic or technical questions which have absorbed so much of our energy in the past. If the meaning of conditional acceptance of deterrence is that it provides time and space for political change to occur, then the 1990s may offer the best possibility we have had for such a change since the beginning of the nuclear age.

Both the strategy of deterrence and the philosophy of arms control have been based on the premise of an unyielding, irreconcilable conflict between the United States and the Soviet Union. Deterrence was designed to identify the common ground we share in our mutual vulnerability to nuclear retaliation. Arms control was designed to render that common vulnerability more stable, less open to accident or misperception, and, if possible, less costly. Stability—whether crisis stability, arms race stability, or political stability—was the highest goal one could hope to achieve in this unending competition.

In a world of over 50,000 nuclear warheads, stability remains a worthy and necessary objective of policy. It would be foolhardy not to continue the pursuit of stability as I have defined it.

In the 1990s, it would be equally foolish to confine our vision, our policy, or our hopes only to stability. The premises of the past in the superpower competition may not serve us well in the future. Today, respected analysts of the U.S.–Soviet relationship tell us that possibilities exist to transform the content of the political relationship between the superpowers. In the past, the political context was regarded as immutable, locked in endless conflict. The best one could do was to make the competition safer.

Today, many believe we should give priority attention to the political issues over the strategic questions. The premise here would be to test whether changes in the political relationship could open the way for deeper and broader control over strategic weapons than we had ever thought possible in the past.

In my view, this direction of stressing the possibilities of political change—testing them stringently but vigorously and boldly—is precisely what conditional acceptance of deterrence implies. The primacy of the political over the strategic, the possibilities of seeking fundamental changes in the superpower relationship—these are the themes which should be stressed in the 1990s.

This is the direction espoused by Pope John Paul II in his encyclical, *On Social Concern*, of 1988, when he argued that it is time to overcome "the logic of blocs" in world politics. Obviously, this Pope is hardly naive about the East–West relationship. But he joins respected, careful analysts in our own country, such as George Kennan, who sense the possibilities of change and, therefore, the moral imperative to test those possibilities with all the wisdom and political imagination we can generate in this society.

To stress the political is not to ignore the strategic relationship. The most rapid political change one could realistically imagine would leave hundreds, perhaps thousands, of nuclear weapons on each side of the East–West divide. It would also leave a world in which the proliferation of nuclear arsenals to other countries will be a more pressing problem in the 1990s than it has been in the past decade.

Taking the strategic dimension seriously means moving forward in those areas of arms control which show promise. We should be able in this decade to accomplish deep cuts in offensive weapons in START, to continue the restraint on defensive systems which has served us well under SALT I, and to open the way for the first serious initiatives on conventional arms control in the last thirty years.

The political possibilities before us are complementary to the strategic imperatives of arms control. To press the political possibilities as our priority may open opportunities for control of the arms race that have previously escaped us. To make progress on specific strategic measures of control can mean enhancing the atmosphere of the political relationship.

The ethics of deterrence in the 1990s will have an ethic of both politics and strategy. The moral vision required in the next decade should build on the work of the 1980s, but it needs to be broader and deeper than the ethic of the control of weapons outlined above. It must be an ethic which can support and sustain precisely those alternatives to the present security system which go beyond deterrence and beyond the Cold War which generated and continued the deterrence relationship.

The questions of the 1960s to the 1980s will not go away. But there are new questions and new possibilities before us in the 1990s. It will take a combination of political, strategic, and moral vision to grasp the opportunities before us. I believe that, as a society, we are capable of doing so. But it will take the kind of serious effort which this conference exemplifies to develop the vision needed for the 1990s.

The time is ripe; the need is urgent. I commend you, therefore, for the initiative you have taken, and I pray that your deliberations during these days will help to shape this new vision.

The Consistent Ethic of Life after Webster

Woodstock Theological Center
Georgetown University
March 20, 1990

I wish to express my appreciation to Fathers O'Donovan and Connor for inviting me to return to Georgetown. It is always a pleasure to come, although I do not envy your students. At least in my case, you have a genius for assigning very difficult topics. In 1984, in the midst of the presidential campaign, you asked me to lecture on religion and politics. This time, you suggested the topic, "The Consistent Ethic of Life after *Webster.*"

The title really contains two themes which I will not treat equally. On the one hand, it calls for assessment of the status and role of the consistent ethic of life. On the other, it focuses the discussion on one issue in the ethic, abortion, in light of the Supreme Court's decision of last July. I will explore the second topic at greater length, but in the context of the consistent ethic.

Specifically, I plan to (1) review the consistent ethic of life since 1983, (2) examine the abortion issue since *Webster,* and (3) close with a perspective on the future of the consistent ethic.

I. The Consistent Ethic Since 1983

The idea of the consistent ethic grew from a conviction I developed as chairman of both the committee which prepared *The Challenge of Peace* and the Committee on Pro-Life Activities. These two distinct efforts seemed to share a common goal. It struck me that the age-old task of the Church, to protect and promote human life as a gift and trust from God, faced in our time a series of threats and challenges of a different magnitude than the past. The new challenge was a product of "the signs of the times" in the sense that technological change, growing global interdependence, and the complexity of an advanced industrial society

79

brought several new challenges to life and some very old ones together in one large problematic. I thought it would be useful to begin a discussion about the utility of relating problems without submerging one into another. How does the experience look after seven years? I will comment briefly on selected moral issues: where we stand, and what needs to be done.

The Nuclear Threat: The danger of nuclear war, perhaps more than any other single issue, symbolizes the new character of threats to life in the 20th century. In the words of McGeorge Bundy's recent history, the Cold War has been played out between "danger and survival." Since political change was judged impossible, the best to be hoped for was strategic stability. In the pastoral letter on war and peace, our hope was for a mix of arms control measures and modest political changes to transform gradually the world we have known for almost fifty years.

However, the last two years have produced anything but modest change. Today, the possibility exists to reshape the U.S.–Soviet relationship in a fashion which would dramatically transform the nuclear relationship. There are still 50,000 nuclear weapons to be reduced, and a consistent ethic should contribute to the changing political and strategic drama we are experiencing. But the hope of the pastoral letter, radical reduction in the danger we have known and the possibility of a different political order in world affairs, is closer at hand than I would have ever guessed in 1983.

Capital Punishment: The consistent ethic's opposition to capital punishment is rooted in the conviction that an atmosphere of respect for life must pervade a society, and resort to capital punishment does not enhance this attitude. In contrast to the nuclear question, a brief report on this topic must be starkly negative. The number of men and women condemned to die grows each year; the general public does not share the conviction of the consistent ethic on capital punishment; and we have recently had the spectacle of people running for public office on the basis of whom they are prepared to kill.

Even though the Catholic tradition, in principle, allows states to resort to capital punishment, and in spite of the public consensus which presently exists, I am convinced that a consistent ethic cannot change on this question. But we must be prepared for a long, strenuous effort with no solid hope for early progress.

Euthanasia: Complementing a willingness to kill criminals to solve crime is the call to legalize euthanasia in our society. By no means do I wish to collapse these two different questions. I only want to point toward a troubling attitude which seems to hold that killing—whether done in an official act or even from a humanitarian motive—only affects the victim. A consistent ethic points out how killing can erode our societal reverence for human life, our bonds of trust, and our respect for one another. A society which is willing to make killing a normal solution for life's problems misunderstands its corrosive effect. Euthanasia may well be the abortion debate of the 1990s, dividing us again as a people over how life in its vulnerability is to be cared for. In 1983, euthanasia was a passing reference in the list of threats to life. It will be more central, I fear, in our future.

Social and Economic Justice: The consistent ethic joined the task of protecting life to that of promoting life. If life is to be respected in a society as a whole, it must be protected in its most vulnerable members. Centuries ago, the prophets taught Israel that the quality of its faith could be tested by how the widows and orphans were treated. These were the inhabitants on the edge of the circle of life in Israel. Jesus specified the message more dramatically. Those at the edge of the circle—the vulnerable and the broken—were very special to God, he said, and, indeed, God was found among them in a particular way.

Almost two millennia later, the prophetic message about the widows and orphans sounds starkly contemporary in our society. Today, women and children remain the most vulnerable members of U.S. society. Their lives reflect the persistent social problems of our society: health care, housing, and hunger. We have had a decade of remarkable economic growth, but the prophets would show us where to look, lest we be mesmerized by the illusion that everyone has shared equally in that growth. The consistent ethic of the 1990s will be tested by how the orphans and widows fare.

II. Abortion Since Webster

Having looked at a number of questions which the consistent ethic addresses, I turn now to the abortion issue as it stands after the Supreme Court decision *Webster vs. Reproductive Health Services* in July 1989. To evaluate the status of the abortion question since *Webster,* it is useful to look quickly at the larger picture of abortion since *Roe vs. Wade* and *Doe vs. Bolton* in 1973. Two characteristics stand out: the radical nature of the original decisions, and their divisive impact on our national life.

By the radical character of the 1973 decisions, I mean their profoundly damaging consequences for life and law in U.S. society; these were captured well by two legal scholars, John Noonan in 1973 and Mary Ann Glendon in 1989. Within weeks of the Court's decision, Noonan concisely summarized its impact. Examining how the Court, in its two sweeping decisions, had changed the prevailing consensus of both state law and recent public referenda, Noonan concluded:

> By virtue of its opinions, human life has less protection in the United States today than at any time since the inception of the country. By virtue of its opinions, human life has less protection in the United States than in any country of the Western world.

His judgment, that the results of the *Roe* and *Doe* decisions would isolate the United States in the way it addresses abortion, has now been confirmed in the detailed study of Professor Glendon, *Abortion and Divorce in Western Law*. In an article written just prior to *Webster* in 1989, Professor Glendon observed that "no country in Europe has gone so far as our Supreme Court in permitting abortion on demand."

The radical character of the decision assured a profound and powerful social response. The response has taken shape in the emergence of a national grassroots pro-life/anti-abortion movement, committed to reversing *Roe* and *Doe*; it was born in the 1970s and has sustained the witness for life until today.

Also emergent in the 1970s was a pro-choice/pro-abortion constituency committed to maintaining U.S. law in the position of providing no effective protection to unborn life. The intensity of the public debate, the passions aroused, the positions taken, and the persistence of views cannot be understood without focusing squarely on the underlying issue. As Noonan observed in 1973, *Roe* and *Doe* were analogous to the Dred Scott decision. The aftermath of *Roe* and *Scott* in the Court's history forced this nation to debate and decide who was to be counted as legally protected and fully human.

In the 19th century, the debate centered on black slaves; in the 20th century, on unborn life of every color and nationality. It is hard to conceive of a more fundamental challenge to the moral vision and character of a society: deciding who fits in the circle of the legally protected human community. If we cannot answer that question accurately, with clarity, compassion, and conviction, how can we hope to keep our moral integrity as a people and a nation?

The consistent ethic—both pre- and post-*Webster*—is helpful in that it illustrates the consequences on a range of issues when we fail as a society to protect the sacredness of every human life. A moral vision which does not have room in the circle of the human community for unborn children will inevitably draw the circle of life too narrowly in other decisions of social and economic policy.

Noonan and Glendon have illustrated how we failed in the 1970s to understand the humanity of life at its inception. Others in the 1980s— from the Congressional Budget Office to *America* and *Commonweal*— have documented how we have failed to protect children in terms of infant mortality, health care, nutrition, and housing. The combined judgment of the last twenty years is that both our constitutional policy on abortion and our social policies for women, children, and families have failed to meet minimum standards of justice. There must be a connection—logical, legal, and social—between our lack of moral vision in protecting unborn children and our lack of social vision in the provision of basic necessities for women and children.

The consistent ethic of life seeks to protect and enhance human life from conception to natural death. It is precisely in light of this larger perspective that I find unacceptable the contention that our society has given a responsible answer to the tragedy of abortion in the constitutional regime established by *Roe* and *Doe*. The view that *Roe* is satisfactory contends that its answer has a traditional American character to it: it protects freedom of choice. But this view reduces the compelling moral question—how do we recognize the human among us?—to a procedural problem. The *Roe* rationale asks, "Who decides?" but it does not focus on "What is being decided?" By ignoring the second question, it evades and eviscerates the heart of the moral challenge posed by abortion: not only who is human, but how do we respond to the human when it is vulnerable and voiceless?

As a bishop and a citizen, I cannot passively accept a definition of the fundamental human, moral, and social question posed by abortion which is cast in purely procedural terms. I find myself responding here as I have when the threat posed by the nuclear arms race is discussed solely in terms of the technical characteristics of missiles and warheads, with the human reality suppressed and ignored. The abortion question must be addressed within the Church and society in terms of its full human substance. There is more to this question than the mere phrase "freedom to choose" can capture. The substance of the issue must be argued at the moral, legal, and political levels.

The post-*Webster* period gives our society the opportunity to do precisely this. *Webster*'s significance is not that it reversed *Roe,* but that it returns the democratic process to the fifty states and gives them the opportunity to redress the faulty logic of *Roe.* It allows the public debate to focus on *what is being decided* in an atmosphere dominated by the question, *who decides.*

For the Church and for the consistent ethic, there are both *opportunities* and *dangers* in this post-*Webster* era.

We have the *opportunity*—by our witness, advocacy, persuasion, and arguments—to make a positive contribution to the national debate on abortion. We hope we can help our society turn away from abortion and save the lives of millions of our unborn sisters and brothers. We have the opportunity to be a consistent and constant defender of human life and dignity, a teacher of the truth that every life is precious—no matter how young or old, how rich or poor, no matter what race or sex or status in society.

But there is also the *danger* that we could make the mistake of some of the pro-abortion groups and narrow our public concern to a single issue, ignoring other threats to human life. There is the danger we might become increasingly shrill or strident, forgetting the importance of civility and charity in public discourse. There is the temptation simply to proclaim positions, forgetting that, in a pluralistic society, we must persuade, build coalitions, and reach out to shape public opinion to support human life. And there is the temptation to lose hope, to give up, to turn away in frustration, apathy, or discouragement.

I have been disappointed in the public dialogue since *Webster* because so much attention has been focused on protest and power, and so little to what is at stake substantively for our society. The basic question is the kind of society we want to be—one that destroys its unborn children, or one that commits itself to a decent life for the most vulnerable in our midst, especially women and children. This fundamental question must be addressed *morally, legally,* and *politically.*

At the *moral* level, the first challenge of the post-*Webster* period is to redress the consequences of *Roe*'s definition of the abortion issue. Redress means lifting up for evaluation the forgotten factor in *Roe,* the moral meaning of unborn life; in technical terms, the moral status of fetal life. This implies asking what moral claims the unborn child has on us. The claims cannot simply be on the mother of the unborn child, but on society as well. Catholic teaching has always seen in the abortion decision a personal and a social choice. The damage done in abortion is not simply to the unborn child, but also to the society which permits, sustains, or encourages abortion. Raising up the forgotten factor of *Roe* means reexamining publicly why life which is demonstrably human in its genetic character and development can be denied all legal protection for six months and any effective legal protection until birth.

The challenge for the consistent ethic in the post-*Webster* period is to make an effective case in our society for Pope John Paul II's assertion that the right to life is the fundamental human right. A consistent ethic will ask, What happens to other rights in a society when protection of the right to life is selective? What happens to our moral imagination and social vision if the right to life is not protected for those who do not look fully human at the beginning or end of life? What happens to the vulnerable along the full spectrum of life, if the right to life is denied to inherently vulnerable and dependent unborn life?

Precisely because of this forgotten factor in *Roe*'s definition of the abortion issue, a consistent ethic must assert with moral creativity and courage Vatican II's statement that "from the moment of conception life must be guarded with the greatest care."

It is my conviction that the strength of the Catholic moral tradition, its persistent defense of unborn life, responds directly to the needs of the post-*Webster* moment—redressing the exclusion of concern for the unborn in *Roe*. But I also want to face directly the critique which contends that, in our emphasis on the forgotten factor of *Roe*, we have ignored the problems faced by women.

Those who espouse a pro-life, consistent ethic—whether they be bishops or laity, authors or activists—need to address this critique very carefully. Our necessary—indeed, essential—public witness in providing a place in the public debate for the moral claims of unborn children can lead to a failure to address the situations faced by pregnant women. We can fail to consider the circumstances of conception—that it can be the result of coercion, ignorance, or abuse. We can seem to be unaware that women who want to bear their children are without the social and economic resources needed to sustain new life. We can appear to ignore the fact that pregnancy for some women is at least partly the experience of being left alone with the consequences of immoral, irresponsible male behavior—at the point of conception and afterwards. These issues, the circumstances surrounding conception and the resources needed to sustain a pregnancy and support children, are also part of the moral fabric of the abortion debate.

A pro-life, consistent ethic acknowledges the human and moral significance of these questions. It must respond to them at the levels of both moral analysis and social support. At the moral level, we should acknowledge the human complexity of many abortion decisions, but we should stress that the key to sound moral analysis is *how* the several moral elements of a complex situation are ranked and related to a decision. To acknowledge the moral weight of the circumstances of conception, and the challenge of sustaining a pregnancy, does not mean one has to accept the direct killing of innocent life as a solution. A consistent ethic challenges this conclusion and indicts it for its failure of social vision and moral courage.

The indictment is not directed in the first instance to the woman caught in these circumstances, but to a social policy and vision fostered since *Roe,* which presents abortion as the normal, natural response to the circumstances I have described. The consistent ethic must stand morally and socially against such a response. We should be second to none in our sensitivity to the problems pregnant women face. But we should offer a different moral response for individuals and society at large. Basing our position on Vatican II's judgment that abortion is an "unspeakable crime," we must combine moral wisdom with specific social policies of health care, housing, nutrition, and counseling programs in our own institutions. We must also support public programs which provide an alternative to the hard and narrow choices pregnant women often face.

But a moral position alone is inadequate for the post-*Webster* period. The essential challenge we face is that unborn life is deprived of even minimal legal protection. Another key post-*Webster* question is: By what civil law shall our society be guided?

I have argued earlier that Catholic teaching sees in abortion a double moral failure: a human life is taken, and a society allows or supports the killing. Both concerns, protecting life and protecting the society from the consequences of destroying lives, require attention. Both fall within the scope of civil law. Civil law, of course, is not co-extensive with the moral law which is broader in its scope and concerns. But the two should not be separated; the civil law should be rooted in the moral law even if it should not try to translate all moral prohibitions and prescriptions into civil statutes.

When should the civil law incorporate key moral concerns? When the issue at stake poses a threat to the public order of society. But at the very heart of public order is the protection of human life and basic human rights. A society which fails in either or both of these functions is rightfully judged morally defective.

Neither the right to life nor other human rights can be protected in society without the civil law. To hold the moral position of the Catholic

Church—that all directly intended abortion is morally wrong—and not to relate this moral position to civil law would be a grave abdication of moral responsibility. Precisely in a pluralistic society, where moral views differ, protection of fundamental rights is directly dependent upon the content of the civil law. In our society we cannot depend on moral agreement alone; the fact of our pluralism means that the content of civil law, what binds us all on essential social questions, is a major public concern.

But does this imply that we are imposing our religious beliefs on society as a whole? No, for two reasons. First, in making the case for a reversal of *Roe* and a legal order which protects the unborn, we present our views in terms of the dignity and the quality of human life, the bond between human dignity and human rights, and the conviction that the right to life is the fundamental human right. Second, our objective, that the civil law recognize a basic obligation to protect human life, especially the lives of those vulnerable to attack or mistreatment, is not new in our society. The credibility of civil law has always been tested by the range of rights it defends, and the scope of the community it protects. To return to the analogy of civil rights: The struggle of the 1960s was precisely about extending the protection of the law to those unjustly deprived of protection. The people of the United States did not need a religious consensus to agree on this proposition then; they do not need religious agreement today to understand the argument that a part of the human community is without fundamental protection of the law.

The extent or kind of legal protection that can be achieved for unborn children is partly dependent on the degree of public consensus which can be built to sustain a legal norm. Since civil law does not incorporate the moral law *in toto*, to build such a consensus, a convincing case must be made that abortion *is* a public order issue.

Pro-life constituencies, including the Catholic bishops, but not limited to them, have pursued two approaches to the civil law. At the constitutional level, for example, the bishops have supported and continue to pursue a constitutional amendment which would protect the life of the unborn child. This is a response as fundamental and far-reaching in scope as the *Roe* decision was. While the effort continues, there is much work to be done in terms of public opinion. A second approach has been to seek limits on abortions, even with *Roe* in place. Obviously, the *Webster* decision offers a new range of possibilities at the state level for this strategy. Moreover, there are solid public opinion grounds for pursuing a regime of limitation on abortions.

This pursuit, however, moves the abortion debate from the moral and legal levels to the *political*. New questions arise for the Church at this level: Should the consistent ethic be pursued in the political process—in the world of party platforms, campaigns, specific legislation, and an examination of the positions of public officials and candidates for public office?

There are two reasons why the Church—keeping within proper theological and constitutional bounds—should engage the issues of the consistent ethic in the political process. *First,* with regard to the abortion question, the democratic process is the arena where we may be able to close the gap between the consequences of the *Roe* decision and the consistently expressed views of U.S. citizens. In polling data, it is clear that the regime of permissive abortion established by *Roe* and expanded by later Court decisions does not reflect a consensus in the public. While public views on abortion are often described as ambiguous, the ambiguity does not diminish the dissatisfaction with 1.5 million abortions a year. Let me simply summarize some data:

- In Connecticut Mutual Life's extensive survey of American values in the 1980s, 65% of U.S. citizens considered abortion morally wrong. Particularly significant was the finding that women, racial minorities, and the poor opposed abortion more strongly than 65%.
- In a *Newsweek*/Gallup poll last Fall, 88% of U.S. citizens favored informed consent for women seeking abortions; 75% favored parental notification for teenagers; 61% favored prohibitions on public funding of abortions except in life-threatening circumstances.
- In the *New York Times* a month after *Webster,* 71% favored parental consent laws and 60% favored testing for fetal viability.

In a debate as complex and emotional as abortion, statistics can be used and abused. I wish only to make a basic point: The status quo of permissive abortion does not fit the moral or legal convictions of a large majority of U.S. citizens. They may not be where the Catholic bishops are, but neither are they where *Roe* and *Doe* left us.

Webster offers an opportunity to use the democratic process to translate a significant consensus on key limits to abortion into law. To grasp the opportunity of a post-*Webster* period, we need to join firm convictions about what is right and wrong at the moral level with a capacity to build a consensus at the legal level that will significantly reduce the number of abortions. We should join others—believers and humanists, Christians and Jews—who share the view that 1.5 million abortions a year is unacceptable for even one more year.

I am convinced that a potential exists which has not yet been grasped; the potential lies in the 60% of Americans who do not identify themselves completely with either of the major voices in the abortion debate. Without forsaking our moral principles, we should seek to address this constituency in a way that invites them to join us in setting significant limits on abortion. To do so will require clarity of moral vision on our part; it will also demand a capacity for creative choices to build consensus at the level of law and policy. It will also require that we raise the quality of the public debate on abortion from rhetoric to rational dialogue even as we seek to reduce the quantity of abortions performed.

The *second* reason the Church should pursue the consistent ethic in the political process is that religious institutions in a democracy stand at the intersection of public opinion and public policy decisions. In a complex democracy like ours, public opinion seldom translates directly into policy decisions. But it does set a framework for policy decisions. It sets limits for policy choices and provides indications of policies desired by the public.

The Church influences this intersection of opinion and policy through its access to the conscience of citizens. In the first instance, this will be the conscience of Catholics, but the U.S. bishops' pastoral letters showed that it is possible to gain a hearing beyond the confines of the Church.

Within the Church, teaching on moral and social policy is addressed to the community as believers and as citizens. Within the community, some citizens will carry specific professional or vocational responsibilities on certain issues. When we wrote the pastoral letter on peace, we addressed it to the citizens of a nuclear nation, but we were conscious of the specific responsibilities and choices faced by Catholics in the military. When we wrote the letter on the economy, we held special meetings with labor and business leaders. On health care issues, physicians, nurses, and administrators have unique choices to face, and special witness to offer.

Finally, there is the position of Catholics holding public office. In a sense, all of the above issues and more are encompassed in the decisions public officials must make. As you know, the question of Catholic political leaders and the abortion question was included in a resolution from the General Meeting of the National Conference of Catholic Bishops last

November. My purpose a moment ago was simply to put it in the context of professional choices made by others in the Church. Now I will apply it to Catholic political leaders, offering here my personal interpretation of these issues.

The relevant text from the bishops reads:

> At this particular time, abortion has become the fundamental human rights issue for all men and women of good will . . . No Catholic can responsibly take a "pro-choice" stand when the "choice" in question involves the taking of innocent human life.

I wish to make ten points on this sensitive issue.

1. Note that the bishops' text is addressed to *all* Catholics, not only to political leaders.

2. Its basic purpose is to state clearly the Church's objective moral teaching. Because all directly intended abortions are judged immoral in Catholic teaching, a pro-choice public policy—which, in effect, is pro-abortion—collides directly with this moral teaching. In this specific judgment of moral and legal precepts, the bishops could hardly have stated their principles any differently.

3. While public officials are bound to fulfill their offices in light of a given constitutional framework, they obviously have some room for specific choices within that framework and can choose to emphasize some issues over others.

4. In accord with the bishops' statement, I am firmly committed to the position that public officials who recognize the evil of abortion have a responsibility to limit its extent, to work for its prevention, and to protect unborn life.

5. I am also firmly convinced that *all* Catholics are bound by the moral principle prohibiting directly intended abortion. However, many Catholics, politicians and ordinary citizens, will disagree on strategies of implementation to lessen and prevent abortions. At the level of strategy and tactics, we bishops should express views as we did in the pastoral letters. By definition, these views are open to debate.

6. The relationship of moral principle, civil law, and public policy is complex. We should encourage and foster an ongoing conversation within the Church about strategies to address abortion.

7. While public consensus is needed to support law, consensus must be created by many voices, including public officials who can try to move

the public toward a better moral consensus. Neither church leaders nor politicians should simply wait for consensus to form.

8. The position of a public figure who is personally opposed to abortion, but not publicly opposed in terms of any specific choices, is an unacceptable fulfillment of a public role. I do not pretend to know in every circumstance which tactics such a figure should use, but moral consistency requires that personal conviction be translated into some public actions in order to validate the personal view. Sometimes public officials may be faced with a dilemma, for example, when they must decide whether to support a law which may not be in total accord with their moral convictions, but would nonetheless decrease the number of abortions. In such a situation, they must ultimately decide which is the better course of action.

9. I have always believed dialogue with public officials—Catholics and others—is an essential part of the Church's social ministry. Moreover, *all* public officials should be held accountable for their positions. Indeed, there are times when criticism is called for. It is important, however, that we continue to engage them and not cut them off.

10. The Church's teaching authority is ultimately a moral authority, a wisdom to be shared with all its members. I believe that the Church can be most effective in the public debate on abortion through moral persuasion, not punitive measures.

III. The Future of the Consistent Ethic

I return now—all too briefly because of the length of my presentation—to the consistent ethic. In assessing its future role, I will speak to questions of both *substance* and *style*.

In terms of *substance*, I remain convinced after seven years of experience that its original premise remains valid. It was proposed to help and urge the Church to keep our moral perspective broadly designed, to address issues on their intrinsic merits, but also to recognize that the life issues today are not confined to one area of human activity. It was also designed to draw upon the systematic resources of the Catholic moral tradition. We are not a single-issue tradition or a single-issue Church; we enhance our treatment of each issue by illustrating its relationship to others.

This general conviction, that the substance of the consistent ethic complements both the signs of our times and the strength of the Catholic tradition, is reinforced by the topic I have addressed at length this evening. In the polarized setting of the abortion debate, it is still possible to locate the majority of Americans as the broad middle, generally opposed to abortion on demand, but ambiguous about how many restrictions to place upon it. Neither the pro-life nor the pro-choice positions have moved this middle toward a viable political and civil consensus.

To convince this 60% of the populace of the wisdom of at least limiting abortion would be a major advance for life. I am convinced that moving the middle depends upon projecting a broad-based vision which seeks to support and sustain life. It will not be enough to be against abortion; we need to show convincingly that we are *for life*—life for women and children; *for life,* in support of the very old and the very young; *for life,* which enhances the chance for the next generation to come to adulthood well-educated, well-nourished, and well-founded in a value structure which provides a defense against the allure of drugs, violence, and despair.

I believe that the work of the Campaign for Human Development, Catholic Charities, Catholic Relief Services, and the many other initiatives we sponsor around the country give us a start, an opportunity to project this vision persuasively. The consistent ethic gives us a way both to propose the vision and to pursue it.

The substance of the consistent ethic yields a *style* of teaching it and witnessing to it. The style should be prophetic, but not sectarian. The word "prophetic" should be used sparingly and carefully, but a truly consistent ethic of word and deed, which protects life and promotes it, is truly a work of God, hence a prophetic word in our time. Such a vision and posture inevitably will meet resistance. But we should resist the sectarian tendency to retreat into a closed circle, convinced of our truth and the impossibility of sharing it with others. To be both prophetic and public, a countersign to much of the culture, but also a light and leaven for all of it, is the delicate balance to which we are called.

The style should be persuasive, not preachy. We should use the model of *Gaudium et spes,* the Second Vatican Council's Pastoral Constitution on the Church in the Modern World: We should be convinced we have much to learn from the world and much to teach it. We should be confident but collegial with others who seek similar goals but may differ on means and methods. A confident Church will speak its mind, seek as a community to live its convictions, but leave space for others to speak to us, help us to grow from their perspective, and to collaborate with them. May my words this evening contribute to this confidence.

The Challenge of Peace—1993

Norwich, Connecticut
May 1, 1993

In early May, 1983, the U.S. Catholic bishops met at the Palmer House in Chicago to give final approval to the third draft of their pastoral letter, *The Challenge of Peace: God's Promise and Our Response*. Bishop Reilly was a member of the ad hoc committee which produced the draft, and I was its chairman. If a reporter had asked us to speculate on what the world would look like in the next ten years, none of us would have predicted or even imagined the enormous changes that have taken place in the past decade.

In 1983, Cold War politics and geo-strategic posturing were feeding an arms race which was the subject of debate throughout the world. The leaders of the two superpowers had not met for four years, and there was considerable pessimism about the possibility of improving relations between the two nations.

In 1993, there is a totally new context for a pastoral statement on war and peace. The Soviet Union has been dismantled, and the Cold War has ended. But regional conflicts have resurged, fed by ethnic and historic tensions. The time is ripe, therefore, to address the unfinished business of the pastoral letter, that is, the challenges of peacemaking and solidarity in a changed, new world.

This morning, I will base my presentation on three episcopal conference projects in which I have personally participated: the pastoral letter itself, the report of an ad hoc committee of bishops appointed to reassess the positions articulated in the pastoral letter in the light of new developments between 1983 and 1988, and the task before the current Ad Hoc Subcommittee on the Tenth Anniversary of *The Challenge of Peace*.

1. The Challenge of Peace

The Challenge of Peace reflects the rich character of the Church's extensive body of teaching on international relations. It attends to three concerns within the encompassing framework of global order and nuclear realities:

economic justice, human rights, and the use of force. As such, the letter exemplifies the application of the Catholic social tradition by a national episcopal conference.

Given the empirical context within which we framed the document, the letter treats the issues and policy questions of the early 1980's. Most notable to the media were issues with political implications. Many still recall the public attention which the third draft's use of the word "curb" in place of "halt" received in our recommendation on the testing, production, and deployment of new nuclear weapons systems.[15] Pastoral and theological issues, however, were the central focus of *The Challenge of Peace*. It is particularly disappointing that Chapter Three, "The Promotion of Peace: Proposals and Policies" and Chapter Four, "The Pastoral Challenge and Response" have been widely neglected in the past decade.

As the introduction stated, "Apprehension about nuclear war is almost tangible and visible today." Bringing the resources of the Catholic tradition to bear on the debate on public policy had a secondary purpose of articulating clearly and convincingly the substance of this tradition and the manner in which the Church should witness to it.

An analysis of *The Challenge of Peace* in the light of the Church's tradition on war and peace must consequently address both the political and the pastoral dimensions of the issues. I will comment on two issues discussed in the pastoral: our approach to nuclear weapons, and our consideration of the pacifist and just war strands of our tradition.

In regard to our approach to nuclear weapons, the pastoral letter clearly stated our intentions:

> The task before us is not simply to repeat what we have said before; it is first to consider anew whether and how our religious-moral tradition can assess, direct, contain, and we hope, help to eliminate the threat posed to the human family by the nuclear arsenals of the world. (#122)

With this in mind, *The Challenge of Peace* scrutinized the questions raised for the Church in one of the two nuclear superpowers.

The pastoral letter's framework for the consideration of the issues surrounding nuclear weapons was shaped by the Church's tradition. Besides employing categories of moral analysis found in papal teaching, it also incorporated two characteristic strands of it. On the one hand, the letter offered a prophetic critique of the nuclear arms race, inveighing against it because of the threat it poses to the world as well as the cost it exacts even if the weapons are never used. On the other hand, the letter mirrored the Holy See's cautious and carefully drawn approach to arms control and disarmament. This led to the careful consideration of nuclear policy.

In evaluating policy, *The Challenge of Peace* applied appropriate elements of the tradition to questions of the use of nuclear weapons and the policy of deterrence. Just war criteria directly and categorically ruled out counter-population warfare, determined that no situation legitimating the initiation of nuclear war could be perceived, and questioned whether limited nuclear war could really be waged.

The question of deterrence, however, was not so easily resolved. The pastoral letter concluded that deterrence can be accorded only a "strictly conditioned moral acceptance."[16] In other words, deterrence must be seen, as Pope John Paul II has said, "not as an end in itself but as a step on the way toward progressive disarmament."[17] Proposals for a nuclear arsenal that are based on strategies of prolonged nuclear war or on winning a nuclear war are unacceptable, as are efforts to establish superiority in nuclear capacity. These conclusions led to prudential judgments that have a level of specificity that papal and conciliar teaching appropriately does not have.

While papal teaching does not discuss specific public policies, it does provide certain procedural criteria with respect to disarmament questions. The pastoral letter considered its policy options within the framework of these criteria. In its recommendations to halt the development of new nuclear weapons systems, to support deep bilateral cuts in nuclear arsenals, and to enhance control over deployed weapons, the letter scrupulously abides by the criteria that disarmament be gradual, controlled, guaranteed, and bilateral. *The Challenge of Peace* thus follows the logic of the tradition and takes it to a level appropriate for the local church.

In constructing the framework for the consideration of these policy questions, *The Challenge of Peace* had to handle a pastoral question that reemerged incisively in the nuclear age: specifically, the relationship between the pacifist and the just war dimensions of the Church's tradition.

The historical context in which *The Challenge of Peace* was written demanded greater clarity in the ethical constructs needed to face the contemporary issues of war and peace. For some, the horrible destructiveness of modern warfare raised questions about the adequacy of traditional moral categories in guiding ethical reflection. The Church's teaching itself had expanded to affirm the right of individuals to opt for conscientious objection.[18] With *Gaudium et Spes* as a point of departure, the U.S. bishops' reflection on the Vietnam War led many to the conclusion that Catholics could claim conscientious objector status, both generally and selectively. Change, both in the Church and in the world, precipitated a new appraisal not only of war itself, but also of our manner of reflecting on it.

The Challenge of Peace sought to articulate the Church's teaching on war and peace in order to respond to this pastoral need. It concluded that "the new moment" in which we find ourselves sees the just war teaching and the imperative of non-violence as distinct but interdependent methods of evaluating warfare. They may diverge on some specific conclusions, but they share a common presumption against the use of force as a means of settling disputes (# 120). These two approaches may relate paradoxically to each other, but they represent two streams in the tradition which are needed to inform ethical reflection on the current reality.

The melding of pacifism and the just war teaching emphasizes the Christian obligation to defend peace. They differ, not in intent, but in method. *The Challenge of Peace* makes clear that sovereign states do maintain the right to resort to military force for the purpose of self-defense of their own nation or of another nation unable to defend itself against an aggressor. Nevertheless, in an age of advanced technological warfare, the analyses of just war and pacifist moralists often converge in their opposition to deadly methods of warfare. They also join in the insistence that humankind must find non-violent means to resolve international conflicts.

Accordingly, the pastoral letter stressed the importance of diplomacy and encouraged fuller study of non-violent means of resistance to evil. More specifically, it urged the establishment of the U.S. Academy of Peace. These recommendations acknowledge, as the pastoral letter stated that, "non-violent means of fending off aggression and resolving conflict best reflect the call of Jesus both to love and to justice" (# 77).

The Challenge of Peace concluded that both the pacifist and the just war approaches are essential for reflection on war and peace in our time. While there is a tension between the two, this tension holds forth the hope for peace. Accordingly, the bishops said, "We believe the two perspectives support and complement each other, each preserving the other from distortion" (# 121). As we anticipate future world events, we can expect that these two essential dimensions of the Church's teaching on war and peace will help us respond faithfully to our Christian responsibility to defend peace.

2. The 1988 Report of the Ad Hoc Committee

As I stated earlier, in the years since the National Conference of Catholic Bishops adopted *The Challenge of Peace,* changes unforeseen in 1983 have swept over the globe. New questions have emerged, and new challenges confront us. Even before the transformations in Eastern Europe and the former Soviet Union began, the U.S. bishops acknowledged that we must be prepared to update the analysis in the pastoral letter in the light of new international developments. Of particular concern was the assessment of deterrence and the extent to which the conditions set by the pastoral letter were being met.

The need for such a review was apparent soon after the letter was published. The early to mid 1980s was a period of continued escalation in the arms race. Some people called for a total condemnation of deterrence on the grounds that this trend revealed the failure of the deterrence policy to meet the pastoral letter's "strictly conditioned moral acceptance" of the policy. Moreover, just weeks before *The Challenge of Peace* was adopted, President Reagan announced plans for the Strategic Defense Initiative (SDI), which its advocates said would transcend deterrence.

An ad hoc committee of bishops was appointed in November, 1985, to reassess the positions of the pastoral letter. The committee's examination of nuclear policy from 1983 to 1988 reviewed both the troubling developments and promising aspects of the issue.

The most surprising development during this period was the changed climate in regard to arms control. Possibilities not visible when *The Challenge of Peace* was drafted became realities that resulted in the 1987 Intermediate Nuclear Forces (INF) Treaty. This represented a welcome breakthrough in what had been the moribund arms control process and resulted in a relatively small reduction of nuclear weapons. The new impetus in arms control and the bilateral treaty were very much in accord with the criteria of the pastoral letter. This is also true of the Salt II Treaty currently before the Congress and the new Administration.

The Strategic Defense Initiative, meanwhile, significantly changed the terms of the debate on U.S. nuclear policy. Besides altering the climate for arms control talks with the Soviet Union, it presented the ad hoc committee with a new set of questions.

The assessment of SDI was difficult because the stated intention of this weaponry system and its possible consequences were quite different. Its advocates presented SDI as a program that would take us beyond deterrence to a system of nuclear defense. But others charged that this seemingly moral "advance" would, in fact, be a costly destabilizing factor of dubious feasibility and would make nuclear war more likely. The ad hoc committee concluded that, in the final analysis, risks seriously outweighed benefits, and the deployment of SDI would not meet the moral criteria of the pastoral letter.

The committee's report, however, continued to acknowledge the "strictly conditioned moral acceptance" of deterrence. In doing so, the committee neither endorsed the *status quo* nor suggested that progress in arms control and disarmament had been fully satisfactory. On the contrary, it argued that even stronger steps needed to be taken in order to meet the moral criteria of *The Challenge of Peace.*

The rapid changes that made it necessary to reassess the pastoral letter for the period of 1983 through 1988 have been outpaced by more recent events. If no one could predict in 1983 that progress in arms control would occur in the late 1980s, even less could one have foreseen the dramatic transformation that has occurred in Eastern Europe and in East–West relations since Mikhail Gorbachev came to power in the former Soviet Union. One of the dilemmas which ethicists face in the contemporary world is the difficulty of keeping up with technological change. Global political change presents a similar problem for those who seek to apply moral reasoning to international political questions.

3. The Task Before the 1993 Subcommittee

Last year, the U.S. bishops established an Ad Hoc Subcommittee on the Tenth Anniversary of *The Challenge of Peace* to update their fundamental moral assessment of the challenge of peace for the 1990s. This committee, which Bishop Reilly now chairs and of which I am a member, is preparing a statement for consideration at the bishops' meeting in November. This morning, I will note some of the general and specific issues which are engaging the attention of the committee. I will not offer a comprehensive list, nor will I treat the issues in any depth.

From the perspective of 1993, the bishops' two documents, to which I have referred, look very much like texts produced in the 1980's. I find that altogether appropriate, and I will use the concluding section of this address to indicate why the texts of the 1980's took the form they did, and why it is necessary to go beyond these arguments in the 1990s.

Both *The Challenge of Peace* (1983) and *The Report* (1988) were essays on the ethics of "means." This style of analysis is very typical of Catholic moral teaching which has always had a concern for *how* human affairs are conducted as well as what *purposes* are being pursued. While this point locates the analysis of the bishops' documents within a broader framework, it does not fully account for why the documents of the 1980s were so explicitly focused on the means question. This was due in great part to the character of the nuclear debate. The dilemma of the nuclear age, as *The Challenge of Peace* observed, was composed of two elements: a profound political competition between two major states (each representing a comprehensive, but diverse worldview) *and* an ability of each state to use vast nuclear arsenals to defend their interests.

From the mid-1940s through the late 1980s the prevailing political conviction in the West—supported by ample empirical data—was that little if any fundamental progress could be made in reconciling the political divisions of the superpowers. The focus of politics and strategy, therefore, was on the *means* of dealing with the conflict. Specifically, the focus was on joining a conception of strategic doctrine and arms control in a policy which would produce "stability." Stability here primarily meant avoiding nuclear war without sacrificing essential political values; it also meant reducing the possibilities of war by accident or miscalculation; finally, it meant seeking to control (not eliminate) nuclear weapons through negotiations. The bishops' 1983 and 1988 documents were—in the policy sections—an effort to contribute to the political-strategic dialogue on means from the perspective of Catholic moral theology.

The two documents look like texts of the 1980s, not the 1990s, because the changes within the former Soviet Union, in Eastern Europe, and between the United States and Russia have produced the consensus view among analysts, diplomats, and citizens that the Cold War (which the documents of 1983 and 1988 addressed) is over. More specifically, this means that the possibility for shaping *fundamental political change* is now present for the first time in almost fifty years. This possibility is, in turn, reshaping the political, strategic, and moral agenda between the United States and the republics of the former Soviet Union. In the 1990s, fundamental political change is *imperative,* not optional.

The new agenda, in outline form, goes something like this. First, political ethics should precede strategic ethics; relations between the U.S. and Russia and their relations with other nations should be cast in terms of a framework of order, justice, and change in world politics. It is the framework found in Pope John XXIII's *Pacem in Terris,* and in Pope John Paul II's *Sollicitudo Rei Socialis* and *Centesimus Annus.* But the empirical political circumstances of the past made the moral vision seem unreachable. Today, however, this conception of a just order is the precondition for addressing the more specific issues of politics, strategy, and economics. From proliferation to pollution, from deterrence to debt, the demands of world politics today, ethically and politically, require that the conception of order be more fully developed in the light of current circumstances and implemented.

Second, within the primacy of a political ethic, the politics and ethics of means must be pursued with new intensity through arms control. The new political possibilities do not render these hard-core strategic objectives any less urgent. Today, three broad areas of arms control need to be pursued simultaneously: the strategic relationship addressed in the START II Treaty which remains to be ratified; the reduction of Conventional Forces in Europe (CFE) being negotiated; and the long-neglected topic of proliferation, now understood to mean preventing proliferation of nuclear weapons, biological and chemical weapons, and ballistic missiles. The new Chemical Weapons Convention (CWC), which the U.S. signed in January, bans the use, production, stockpiling, and development of chemical weapons—a welcome change from the 1925 Geneva Protocol which merely banned the *use* of chemical weapons in warfare.

Third, the conventional arms trade with and among developing nations needs more attention. The secretary of the Pontifical Council for Justice and Peace has recently indicated that the Council is working on a weapons sales document in order to address this issue. Diverting scarce resources away from the purchase of arms to meeting basic human needs for food, shelter, education, and health care would go a long way toward building a just and peaceful world. At present, there are more than forty regional conflicts, each fueled by an arms trade that knows no bounds. Regional conflicts within and among the republics of the former Soviet Union and among the nations of the former Yugoslavia are especially dangerous, as is the 45-year struggle between Israel and its neighbors. Also especially ominous are the conflicts between India and Pakistan, and between North and South Korea.

The 1990s began with the Iraqi invasion of Kuwait which, in turn, led to the Persian Gulf war. In the months leading up to the outbreak of hostilities on January 17, 1991, most of the world hoped that this crisis would end without resort to the horrors of war. The Church's teaching on war and peace that provided the foundation of *The Challenge of Peace* surfaced as an important ingredient in public debate. The very fact that the just-war criteria played a prominent role in the debate, both before and after the war began, points to another change since 1983. At that time, the public discussion about nuclear weapons specifically, and war in general, focused on political, military, and strategic questions; that has changed, I hope, irrevocably, to include *moral* concerns.

At the same time, doubts remain about whether two of the seven stringent just-war criteria were met in the Persian Gulf war. The first was *proportionality,* which requires that the harm caused—the destructiveness and cost of the war—be proportionate to the good that would be achieved. The costs to be measured are, first, the human lives that would be lost, as well as the ecological, economic, strategic, and even spiritual costs. Particularly reprehensible were the widespread loss of innocent civilian lives and the wholesale destruction of Iraq's infrastructure which is necessary to sustain human life. The second problematic criterion was *last resort,* which means that all other means of resolving the conflict peacefully must have been exhausted. These two criteria, of course, demand that prudential judgments be made about the factual situation; and people of good will may legitimately disagree when making such judgments.

The Persian Gulf war also focused attention on the increasingly sophisticated conventional arms which are readily available throughout the world and have enormous destructive power. This brings to mind Pope John Paul's words at Coventry, England, in the midst of the 1982 war between the British and the Argentines. He said:

Today, the scale and horror of modern warfare, whether nuclear or not, makes it totally unacceptable as a means of settling differences between nations. War should belong to the tragic past, to history; it should find no place on humanity's agenda for the future.

More recently, in *Centesimus Annus,* the Holy Father explained why he rejects the belief that war is inevitable. First, he points to the dramatic revolution in Central and Eastern Europe. The "fall" of the Soviet empire came about, he said, "by means of peaceful protest, using only the weapons of truth and justice." The revolution in the Philippines was also non-violent. Second, the Holy Father cannot morally tolerate the costs of modern warfare. He pleads for peace, saying:

No, never again war, which destroys the lives of innocent people, teaches how to kill, throws into upheaval even the lives of those who do the killing, and leaves behind a trail of resentment and hatred, thus making it all the more difficult to find a just solution of the very problems that provoked war.

Third, the Pope believes that the world has the capacity to develop the resources to handle international disputes as they arise, without recourse to war. Finally, the Holy Father urges that the causes of war be addressed.

He points out that wars always stem from "real and serious grievances." These include poverty, injustice, frustrated aspirations, and exploitation.

In *The Challenge of Peace* we, too, clearly stated there that "the history of recent wars . . . has shown that conventional war can also become indiscriminate in conduct and disproportionate to any valid purpose." (# 217) We added that "we must re-emphasize with all our being . . . that it is not only nuclear war that must be prevented, but war itself." (# 219)

The U.S. bishops' texts of the 1980s give us a starting point for the agenda of the 1990s. But, as I have intimated, it is not sufficient simply to amend the texts of the last decade. They spoke to the questions of the moment; the transition between the 1980s and the 1990s has not been organic. A profound and potentially very hopeful change has occurred. The 1990s is not a time for amending past conceptions; it is a decade which will require fundamental reassessments—politically and morally—of how we can use the transition to the third Christian millennium creatively in pursuit of the values which the social tradition has taught us: peace, justice, truth, love, and freedom.

Part of the agenda of the 1990s is addressing the moral dimensions of such developments as:

- humanitarian intervention in a sovereign state;
- the targeting of homes and infrastructure for bombing and shelling;
- economic sanctions and coercive diplomacy;
- arms embargoes;
- denying food and medicine to civilian populations in order to achieve military objectives;
- the systematic rape of women as an instrument of war;
- the temptation of isolationism;
- international policing.

There is need for new thinking about the status of peace, the nature of war, and effective responses to conflict. There are new questions about the rights and limits of sovereignty.

We must also reassess the role of international institutions like the United Nations. We noted in the *Challenge of Peace* that, "in light of the continuing endorsement found in papal teaching, we urge that the United States adopt a stronger supportive leadership role with respect to the United Nations." (# 268) We added that "it is in the context of the

United Nations that the impact of the arms race on the prospects for economic development is highlighted." (# 269) The end of the Cold War has made it possible for the United Nations to play an important role in reducing tensions and addressing the causes of war. The United States, with the help of the former Soviet Union, was able to build a large coalition of forces to counter Iraq's attempted annexation of Kuwait. The United Nations, with U.S. leadership, also effectively addressed the issue of a starving population in Somalia, although the starvation had reached epidemic proportions before action was taken.

The U.N. has been much less successful in developing an effective restraint on the civil war in Bosnia-Herzegovina. While the Bosnian Serbs stand before the whole world, accused of despicable "ethnic cleansing," European nations, the United States, and the United Nations have been very ineffective in their efforts to relieve the suffering of the Bosnian Muslims and stop their slaughter. As the USCC Administrative Board said weeks ago: "The world cannot stand aside as innocent people are destroyed, as aggression shapes a new world, as the hopes of freedom turn into the violence of war." The Board said there was "no real military solution" to the crisis, and,

> The massive use of military force . . . raises serious problems of proportionality, probability of success, and noncombatant immunity. If force is used, it must be strictly *limited* in its means and objectives; it should *not prolong or widen the war*; and it should *not undermine prospects for a just political solution* to the conflict. In addition, it should be carried out on a *multilateral basis* with the authority of the international community.[19]

Effective steps must be taken to protect the innocent and to stop the horror of ethnic cleansing. The dilemma has been how to prevent further genocide without resorting to unjust means. This question is presently being intensely debated by Congress and the new Administration, as well as in the capitals of Europe.

In the aftermath of the Persian Gulf war, an intriguing question is what impact the Church's teaching on war and peace will have on the major issues that face what some have called a "unipolar" world. The pastoral letter dealt primarily with the nuclear arms race in a *bipolar* environment. We must now turn to the new reality and apply our tradition in ways that continue to seek to minimize the resort to armed force, and indicate the directions we might take to ensure greater justice in the world. The reduction of nuclear arms must continue to be a priority. Nuclear deterrence must continue to give way to progressive disarmament. The growing sophistication and proliferation of conventional arms impels us to redouble our efforts to limit their production and distribution.

Greater attention and resources must also be focused on the growing gap between the Northern and the Southern hemispheres. A just and lasting peace will never be achieved when so many people live in abject poverty.

Peacemaking requires new forms of solidarity in the 1990's. Perhaps, the bluntest way to put this message is the immorality of isolationism. After the Cold War, there is an understandable but dangerous temptation to turn inward, to focus only on domestic needs and to ignore our global responsibilities. But this is not an option for believers in the universal Church nor citizens in the world's last superpower. In a world where 40,000 children die every day from hunger and its consequences; in a world with ethnic cleansing and systematic rape in Bosnia; in a world where people are still denied life, dignity, and fundamental rights because of their race, ethnicity, religion, or economic status—we cannot turn away. As our episcopal conference said last fall:

> Our future in this shrinking world depends not only on our national achievements, but also on global progress. The interests of our nation and the values of our faith are best served by consistent commitment and generous investment in shaping a more just and peaceful world, especially for the poor and vulnerable. Building peace, securing democracy, confronting poverty and despair, and protecting human rights are not only moral imperatives, but also wise national priorities. They can shape a world that will be a safer, more secure and more just home for all of us.

The final chapter of the pastoral letter set forth a challenge for the Church to be a community of conscience, prayer, and penance. It noted that peacemaking is not an optional commitment; it is a requirement of our faith. This is no less true today than it was ten years ago.

When the pastoral letter was being drafted, the fear of nuclear war sparked tremendous interest in what we were doing. This translated into widespread study of the Church's teaching on war and peace, and into an interest in considering the moral dimension of public policy issues. In today's context, we must be committed to advancing further the Church's ministry of peacemaking. And we must do all in our power to engage the attention and interest of the broader community. Returning to "business as usual" would be perilous, for other crises as serious as the one in the Persian Gulf loom on the horizon.

We all share the responsibility for making peace. God has promised us peace. Our challenge is to make that peace a reality. May we not fail to do our part!

The Consistent Ethic of Life and Health Care Reform

National Press Club, Washington, D.C.
May 26, 1994

As many of you may know, in the last year I have experienced a significant amount of press coverage for reasons that are happily behind me. There is a temptation in this prestigious forum to share some of my reactions and reflections based on that experience, but I am going to resist that temptation. At another time and after more reflection on my part, I might share some thoughts about what I learned about the news media and related topics. But today I address a more important and more timely topic—the moral dimensions of health care reform.

For the last decade as a pastor, a bishop, and a leader of our National Conference of Catholic Bishops, I have had the opportunity to address a series of vital moral challenges. I chaired the committee that produced the pastoral letter on war and peace a decade ago. I have served as chair of our bishops' committees on pro-life matters and family-life concerns. As a bishop, I have also seen the crime, injustice, and violence in our neighborhoods and the loss of roots and responsibility in our cities, the loss of the sense of family and caring in our communities that is undermining millions of lives.

I believe that at the heart of so many of our problems—in Chicago and Washington, in Bosnia and Rwanda—there is a fundamental lack of respect for human life and human dignity. Over the past ten years I have articulated a "Consistent Ethic of Life" as a moral framework to address the growing violence in our midst.

The purpose of the consistent life ethic is to provide a moral framework for analysis and motivation for action on a wide range of human life-issues with important ethical dimensions. The consistent life ethic, by design, provides for a public discourse that respects the separation of church and state, and also recognizes the proper role of religious perspectives and ethical convictions in the public life of a pluralistic society.

Over the past years I have addressed many issues in the light of the consistent ethic. In addition to the central question of abortion, I have spoken about euthanasia and assisted suicide, capital punishment, the newer technologies used to assist human reproduction, and war and peace, to name a few. The foundation for all of these discussions is a deep conviction about the nature of human life, namely, that human life is sacred, which means that all human life has an inalienable dignity that must be protected and respected from conception to natural death. For the Christian believer and many others, the source of this dignity is the creative action of God in whose "image and likeness" we are made. Still others are aware that life is a precious gift which must be protected and nurtured.

For advocates of a consistent life ethic, the national debate about health care reform represents both an opportunity and a test. It is an *opportunity* to address issues and policies that are often matters of life and death, such as, who is covered and who is not; which services are included and which are not; will reform protect human life and enhance dignity, or will it threaten or undermine life and dignity? It is a *test* in the sense that we will be measured by the comprehensiveness of our concerns and the consistency of our principles in this area.

In this current debate, a consistent life ethic approach to health care requires us to stand up for both the unserved and the unborn, to insist on the inclusion of real universal coverage and the exclusion of abortion coverage, to support efforts to restrain rising health costs, and to oppose the denial of needed care to the poor and vulnerable. In standing with the unserved and the unborn, the uninsured and the undocumented, we bring together our pro-life and social justice values. They are the starting points for a consistent life agenda for health-care reform.

In these remarks I speak as a pastor of a diverse local church. In Chicago we see both the strengths and the difficulties of our current system. We experience the remarkable dedication, professionalism, and caring of the *people* and the amazing contributions of the *institutions* that make up our health care system. I also see the children without care, the sick without options, the communities without adequate health services, the families and businesses strained and broken by health care costs. We see the hurts and pick up the pieces of a failing system—in our hospitals and clinics, our shelters and agencies, our parishes and schools. We look at health care reform from the bottom up, not who wins or loses politically, not how it impacts powerful institutions and professions, but how it touches the poor and vulnerable, the unserved and the unborn, the very young and the very old.

As I indicated earlier, I am also a member of the National Conference of Catholic Bishops, an organization deeply involved in this debate. Our principles and priorities are summarized in a resolution unanimously adopted by the Conference last year (1993).[20] A unanimous vote of our bishops is an unusual accomplishment, as those of you who have ever seen us discuss holy days or liturgical texts can attest! But we found unity in embracing a consistent life ethic approach to health care reform.

The broader health care debate is driven by many factors. For the sake of time, I will list only five without discussing them at any length.

1. The amount of money spent on health care is escalating at an unsustainable rate. It surpassed 14 percent of the gross domestic product (GDP) last year, and it is reasonable to assume that, without effective intervention, it could reach 18% of the GDP by the year 2000.
2. This uncontrolled growth is creating economic hardships for many of our fellow citizens, especially working families.
3. Private insurance programs are deteriorating through risk segmentation into programs that more and more serve those who have the least need for health insurance—the healthy.
4. Cost shifting—that is, the passing on of unreimbursed expenses by health providers to employer premiums—has become a "hidden tax" that no longer is sustainable.
5. Finally, and most significantly, the number of uninsured in the United States continues, now approaching nearly 40 million, a large portion of whom are people who work. Ten million are children. This lack of coverage touches African-American and Hispanic families most directly.

I join the many who have concluded that the United States needs profound systemic change in its health care system. We cannot rely on the system to correct itself. Without intervention, things are getting worse, not better.

I hasten to add that my advocacy is not partisan. Neither do I argue on behalf of any particular proposal before the Congress. I do, however, take exception to those who say that there is no serious systemic problem or that what we face is merely an insurance or a health care delivery problem. On the contrary, there *is* a fundamental health care problem in our nation today. I share this judgment with many leaders of the Catholic community whose outlook and convictions have been shaped

- by the experience of Catholic religious communities and dioceses that operate 600 hospitals and 300 long-term care facilities, constituting the largest non-profit group of health care providers in the United States;
- by the experience of the Catholic Church in the United States, which purchases health coverage for hundreds of thousands of employees and their families;
- by the experience of Catholic Charities, the largest private deliverer of social services in the nation;
- by our experience as a community of faith, caring for those who "fall through the cracks" of our current system.

It is this broad range of experience that led the U.S. Catholic bishops to say last June:

Now is the time for real health care reform. It is a matter of fundamental justice. For so many it is literally a matter of life and death, of lives cut short and dignity denied. We urge our national leaders to look beyond special interest claims and partisan differences to unite our nation in a new commitment to meet the health care needs of our people, especially the poor and the vulnerable. This is a major political task, a significant policy challenge and a moral imperative.

Before addressing some of the more specific issues associated with health care reform, it is important that we consider some even more profound issues. I say this because President Clinton's health care reform proposal and the alternatives to it, like any significant government initiatives that would reorder social relationships and responsibilities, have drawn us into a discussion of fundamental values and social convictions. Several important convictions, which serve as a kind of bedrock for the consistent life ethic, can assist us in this broader discussion. They are:

1. There are *basic goods and values* which we human beings share because we share the gift of human life; these goods and values serve as the common ground for a public morality that guides our actions as a nation and as a society.

2. Within the individual, these common goods and values express themselves in an inalienable human dignity, with consequent *rights* and *duties.*

3. One of the ways these rights and duties are expressed in the human community is through the recognition and *pursuit of the common good*; or, to say it differently, through a good that is to be pursued in common with all of society; a good that ultimately is more important than the good of any individual.

4. This common good is realized in the context of a *living community,* which is nurtured by the virtues and shared values of individuals. Such a community protects the basic rights of individuals.

5. As part of this community, both individuals and institutions (including government, business, education, labor, and other mediating structures) have an *obligation,* which is rooted in distributive justice, to *work to secure this common good*; this is how we go about meeting the reasonable claims of citizens striving to realize and experience their fundamental human dignity.

These convictions find their origin in a vision of the human person as someone who is grounded in community, and in an understanding of society and government as being largely responsible for the realization of the common good. As Catholics we share this vision with many others. It is consistent with fundamental American values, though grounded differently. For example, our Declaration of Independence and our Constitution reflect a profound insight that has guided the development of our nation; namely, that there are certain fundamental human rights that exist before the creation of any social contract (such as the constitution of a sovereign nation), and that these must be protected by society and government. There is an objective order to which we are held accountable and to which we, in turn, hold others accountable in our many relationships and activities. The Catholic tradition also affirms such rights but sees them emerging from the organic relationship between the individual and the community.

As a nation, we also have had a sense of a common good which is greater than the agenda of any individual. Alexis de Tocqueville noted this when he commented on the American penchant for volunteering. We also have been a nation of communities. Whether in the small towns of the Plains or the ethnic communities of the large cities, U.S. citizens had a sense of being bonded together and being mutually responsible. We also recognized that our individual and collective existence is best protected by virtuous living—balancing the demands of personhood and social responsibility. In more recent years, as our social order has become more complex, we have come to see that a proper sense of mutual responsibility requires a greater presence of the state in helping individuals to realize their human potential and social responsibility. Public education and social security are but two examples of this presence.

Without being overly pessimistic, I suggest that these fundamental convictions, which are essential both to a consistent life ethic and to our well-being as a nation and a society, are being challenged today. There is abroad a certain tendency which would suggest that law and public order are accountable only to the subjective convictions of individuals or pressure groups, not to any objective, albeit imperfectly perceived, moral order. Robert Bellah and his associates have convincingly shown how a sense of the common good, the role of community, and the value of virtuous living have been compromised, if not lost, in recent years. I am convinced that the violence that plagues our nation is a symptom of this loss of an overarching social order. We are a nation that is increasingly overly individualistic at the very time when the problems we face require greater common effort and collective responses.

All of this needs to be taken into consideration in any substantive discussion of health care reform. If we are not attentive to issues such as these, then our dialogues and debates will go nowhere because of disagreements—unknown and unacknowledged—on basic principles.

First, there is the issue of *universal access*. In the June 1993 statement I cited earlier, the U.S. Catholic bishops outlined key principles and priorities for initiating and executing reform. Our third principle was universal access to comprehensive health care for every person living in the United States.

We believe that health care—including preventive and primary care—is not only a commodity; it is an essential safeguard of human life and dignity. In 1981, the bishops spoke of health care as a "basic human right which flows from the sanctity of human life."[21] In declaring this, the bishops were not saying that a person had a right to *health*, but that, since the common good is the sum of those conditions necessary to preserve human dignity, one must have a right of *access,* insofar as it is possible, to those goods and services which will allow a person to maintain or regain health. And if one views this right within the context of the convictions I have just discussed, then it is the responsibility of society as a whole and government to ensure that there is a common social order that makes the realization of this good possible. Whether we have health care should not depend on whom we work for, how much our parents earn, or where we live.

So far, so good. Most would agree, at least in theory. Where the disagreement comes is in regard to the last of the convictions I noted in discussing the consistent ethic. Allow me to rephrase it.

> Under the title of distributive justice, society has the obligation to meet the reasonable claims of its citizens so that they can realize and exercise their fundamental human rights.

When many of us Americans think of justice, we tend to think of what we can claim from one another. This is an individualistic understanding of justice. But there is another American instinct which has a broader understanding of justice. It has been summarized by Father Philip Keane, a moral theologian, who wrote: ". . . justice shifts our thinking from what we claim from each other to what we *owe* to each other. Justice is about duties and responsibilities, about building the good community."[22] In this perspective, distributive justice is the obligation which falls upon society to meet the reasonable expectations of its citizens so that they can realize and exercise their fundamental human rights. And, in this instance, the right is that of access to those goods and services that make it possible for persons to maintain their health and thus broaden health care beyond what is provided by a hospital, a clinic, or a physician.

So far I have argued that health care is an essential safeguard of human life and dignity and that there is an obligation for society to ensure that a person be able to realize this right. I now want to go a step further. I believe that the only way this obligation can be effectively met by society is for our nation to make *universal health care coverage* a reality. Universal *access* is not enough. We can no longer tolerate being the only Western nation that leaves millions of persons uncovered. For many, this will be a "hard saying." The cry of political expediency and the maneuvering of special interest groups already are working either to provide a program of access that maintains a two-tiered health care system (which marginalizes large portions of our society) or to limit coverage. When I speak of universal coverage, I do not mean a vague promise or a rhetorical preamble to legislation, but the *practical means* and *sufficient investment* to permit all to obtain decent health care on a regular basis.

If justice is a hallmark of our national community, then we must fulfill our obligations in justice to the poor and the unserved *first* and not last. Similarly, we cannot ignore the millions of undocumented immigrants. Even if the demands of justice were set aside, reasons of public health would necessitate their being included. The undocumented will continue to need medical assistance, and hospitals will continue to be required to provide medical care for those who present themselves for treatment. In a reformed system, which should contain, if not eliminate, the cost-shifting that previously had paid for their care, the medical expenses of the undocumented must be covered for both policy and moral reasons.

Unfortunately, as the national debate on health care reform has evolved, and as legislation has been proposed, an important fact has been lost; namely, that it is not enough simply to expand coverage. If real reform is to be achieved—that is, reform that will ensure quality and cost-effective care—then we must do what is necessary in order to ensure that our health care delivery system is person-centered and has a community focus. Health care cannot be successfully reformed if it is considered only an economic matter. This reform will be morally blighted if the nature of care—something profoundly human, not easily measured, yet that which, far more than technology, remains the heart and breath of the art of healing—is not preserved and expanded along with health coverage itself. The challenge is to provide universal coverage without seriously disrupting the doctor/patient relationship which is so central to good medical care.

After a long period of research and discussion, the Catholic Health Association (CHA) developed a proposal for health care reform that seeks to meet this and other challenges. It is called "Setting Relationships Right." I hope that the values CHA has proposed and the strategies it has developed in this regard will not be lost sight of. Our objective must be a healthy nation where the mental and physical health of the individual is addressed through collaborative efforts at the local level.

Let me summarize my major points so far. First, we need a profound systemic reform of our health care system. Second, justice and the common good demand that this reform include universal coverage. Third, justice at this time requires a program of effective universal coverage that is person-centered and community-based. This leads us to two thorny questions: How is the program to be funded, and how are costs to be contained?

As you know, these two questions are essentially interrelated. It is clear that the rate of cost increases in health care cannot be sustained even if there is no systemic reform. It also is clear that the demands for a more fiscally responsible use of federal monies must be taken into account. We cannot spend what we do not have.

Our episcopal conference has insisted that health care reform must also include effective mechanisms to restrain rising health care costs. Without cost containment, we cannot make health care affordable and direct scarce national resources to other pressing national problems. Containing costs is crucial if we are to avoid dangerous pressures toward the kind of rationing that raises fundamental ethical and equity questions. The poor, vulnerable, and uninsured persons cannot be denied needed care because the health system refuses to eliminate waste, duplication, and bureaucratic costs.

But we may also have to consider other steps to restrain costs and distribute health care more justly. For example, we may have to recognize that basic and preventive care, and health care to preserve and protect life, should be a higher priority than purely elective procedures. This raises the often explosive concept of "rationing." I prefer a different word and a different concept—"stewardship." How do we best protect human life and enhance human dignity in a situation of limited health resources? How do we ensure that the lives and health of the poor and vulnerable are not less valuable or less a priority than the lives and health of the rest of us?

This is not an abstract discussion. Rationing health care is a regular, if unacknowledged, feature of our current health care system. Nearly 40 million are uninsured; 50 million more are underinsured. In 1992, nearly 10 million children were without medical coverage, 400,000 more than in 1991. In my own state of Illinois, 86,000 persons lose their health insurance each month. Being without insurance means being without care when you need it, delaying care until an illness or injury may require more costly intervention or be beyond any treatment.

We now have an insurance model that requires individuals to pay for the items and services which their health care needs require—some without limitations and others with enormous constraints. We have been rationing health care in recent years by squeezing people out of the system through insurance marketing techniques like medical underwriting, pre-existing condition exclusion, and insurance red-lining. Actuarial pricing designed to protect insurance company assets pits one group against another—the old against the young, the sick against the healthy—thus undermining the solidarity of the whole community. We can see this tension playing itself out in the disturbing debates around this country about assisted suicide.

In light of these concerns, the nation must undertake a broad-based and inclusive consideration of how we will choose to allocate and share our health care dollars. We are stewards, not sole owners, of all our resources, human and material; thus, goods and services must be shared. This is not a task for government alone. Institutions and individuals must be involved in reaching a shared moral consensus, which will allow us to reassert the essential value of the person as an individual and as a member of the community. From that moral consensus must come a process of decision-making and resource allocation which preserves the dignity of all persons, in particular the most vulnerable. It is proper for society to establish limits on what it can reasonably provide in one area of the commonweal so that it can address other legitimate responsibilities to the community. But in establishing such limits, the inalienable life and dignity of every person, in particular the vulnerable, must be protected.

The Catholic Health Association has addressed the ethics of rationing and offered some moral criteria. These demand that any acceptable plan must meet a demonstrable need, be oriented to the common good, apply to all, result from an open and participatory process, give priority to disadvantaged persons, be free of wrongful discrimination, and be monitored in its social and economic effects.

This kind of framework offers far better guidance than the moral bankruptcy of assisted suicide and the ethically unacceptable withholding of care based on "quality of life" criteria. We will measure any cost containment initiative by two values: Does it distribute resources more justly? And does it protect the lives and dignity of the poor and vulnerable?

But the problem of rationed access to necessary medical care is only one aspect of the cost containment debate. What of the issue of *funding*? Obviously I cannot offer a detailed analysis of the specific proposals which are on the table. But I can say this: If systemic reform addresses in a substantive manner issues of quality care and cost effectiveness, then justice will demand that all sectors of our society contribute to the support of these efforts. And this support takes two forms. First, each individual must assume appropriate responsibility for the costs associated with health care, and must assume responsibility to do all that is possible not to put his or her health at risk. Second, those segments of our economic order, which have been able to avoid an appropriate level of responsibility for the health care of their employees, must begin to assume their fair share, just as the rest of society must. In other words, we all must be willing to help meet this demand of justice. We must share the sacrifices that will have to be made.

Thus far, I have insisted that a consistent life ethic requires a commitment to genuine universal coverage, because lack of coverage threatens the lives and diminishes the dignity of millions of men, women, and children. I must also say clearly and emphatically that a consistent life ethic requires us to lift the burden of mandated abortion coverage from needed health care reform. I say this for several important reasons:

1. It is morally wrong to coerce millions of people into paying for the destruction of unborn children against their consciences and convictions. How ironic it would be if advocates of "choice," as they call themselves, require me and millions like me to obtain and pay for abortion coverage, which we abhor. It is a denial of "choice," a violation of conscience, and a serious blow to the common good.

2. It is politically destructive. Needed national health care reform must not be burdened by abortion coverage, which neither the country nor the Congress supports. Public opinion polls and recent Congressional action clearly indicate that, whatever their views on the morality or legality of abortion, the American people and their representatives do not wish to coerce all citizens into paying for procedures that so divide our nation. A University of Cincinnati poll in January of this year indicated that only 30% favor the inclusion of abortion as a basic benefit even if it could be included at no cost at all. Only 14% wanted abortion coverage if it would add to the cost of health premiums.

3. Abortion mandates would undermine the participation of Catholic and other religious providers of health care, who now provide essential care in many of the nation's most underserved communities. I fear our hospitals will be unable to fulfill their mission and meet their responsibilities in a system where abortion is a mandated benefit. Strong conscience clauses are necessary to deal with a variety of medical/moral issues, but are not sufficient to protect Catholic and other providers who find abortion morally objectionable. The only remedy is not to link needed reform to abortion mandates.

The sooner the burden of abortion mandates is lifted, the better for the cause of reform. We continue to insist that it would be a grave moral tragedy, a serious policy mistake, and a major political error to link health care reform to abortion. An insistence on abortion coverage will turn millions of advocates of reform into adversaries of health care legislation.

We cannot and will not support reform that fails to offer universal coverage or that insists on abortion mandates. While this offers moral consistency, it can place us in conflicting political alliances. For example, we concur with the position of the President and Mrs. Clinton in calling real universal coverage essential. We concur with Representative Henry Hyde and the pro-life caucus in insisting that abortion coverage must be abandoned. We concur with the Hispanic Caucus in our commitment that universal coverage must be truly "universal coverage."

This is our consistent ethic message to the White House, the Congress, and the country. We are advocates of these key principles and priorities, not any particular plan. We will not choose between our key priorities. We will work with the leaders of our land to pass health care reform, reform that reflects a true commitment to human life and human dignity. As I noted above, the polls indicate that most Americans join us in support for both authentic universal coverage and the exclusion of abortion coverage in health care reform. We will carry this message forward with civility and consistency. We offer our moral convictions and practical experience, not political contributions and endorsements. We have no "attack ads" or PAC funds. But we can be a valuable partner for reform, and we will work tirelessly for real reform without abortion mandates.

For defenders of human life, there is no more important or timely task than offering an ethical and effective contribution to the health care debate. The discussions and decisions over the next months will tell us a lot about what kind of society we are and will become. We must ask ourselves: What are the choices, investments, and sacrifices we are willing to make in order to protect and enhance the life and dignity of all, especially the poor and vulnerable? In the nation's Capital, health care reform is seen primarily as a *political* challenge—the task of developing attractive and workable proposals, assembling supportive coalitions, and securing the votes needed to pass a bill. But fundamentally, health care reform is a *moral* challenge—finding the values and vision to reshape a major part of national life to protect better the life and dignity of all.

Ultimately, this debate is not simply about politics—about which party or interest group prevails. It is about *children* who die because of the lack of prenatal care or the violence of abortion. About *people* who have no health care because of where they work or where they come from. About *communities* without care, and workers without coverage.

Health care reform is both a *political* task and a *moral* test. As a religious community with much at stake and much to contribute to this debate, we are working for health care reform that truly reaches out to the unserved, protects the unborn, and advances the common good.

Euthanasia in the Catholic Tradition

Visiting Scholar Lecture Series
Rockhurst College—Kansas City, Missouri
February 1, 1995

This evening, I will share with you some thoughts on an ethical issue that confronts us in the United States and in many other first world nations. It is paradigmatic of broader cultural or societal movements that have already affected or will impact all of us. I am speaking of the movement to legalize euthanasia or assisted suicide.

I will (1) describe the movement to legalize euthanasia or assisted suicide, (2) offer some reasons why it has become so popular, and (3) examine the issue in the light of the Catholic tradition. Let me begin, however, by clarifying certain terms.

As the U.S. Catholic Bishops pointed out in their Ethical and Religious Directives for Catholic Health Services, approved last November 17, *euthanasia* "is an action or omission which of itself or by intention *causes* death, in order to alleviate suffering." In *assisted suicide* a third party provides the means for a person to kill him- or herself—by lethal injection, a prescription for a lethal drug, or another means. To *cause* death, rather than to *allow* it to occur in the natural course of life, makes all the difference in deciding whether or not a given procedure is euthanasia or assisted suicide. To respect a patient's refusal of treatment or a request to cease treatment is *not* euthanasia. To withdraw or withhold treatment when the burdens are disproportionate to the benefits is *not* euthanasia. To administer medication to relieve pain, even if the foreseen but unintended effect may be to hasten death, is *not* euthanasia. The intention in euthanasia and assisted suicide is to *cause* death, not merely to allow it to happen.

1. The Movement to Legalize Euthanasia

In the United States advocates of euthanasia, or "mercy killing" as it used to be called, have been around for decades. However, up to recently, they have had little impact on our society, its laws, and its public policies. Today, this is rapidly changing—a cause of grave concern for many of us.

One of the reasons for this disconcerting change in attitude stems from the fact that the advocates of euthanasia no longer refer to it as "mercy killing." They now use such ambiguous euphemisms as "aid in dying," similar to the practice of pro-abortion forces in the United States, who prefer to identify themselves simply as "pro-choice." This tactical change has accompanied a growing attention in this country to the plight of families when confronted with a loved one with a debilitating or painful fatal disease as well as to the condition of those who are permanently unconscious, in what is known as a persistent vegetative state.

As a result, three kinds of initiatives have been introduced around the country: (1) state referendums, which, in addition to codifying laudable and appropriate clarifications of the law, have also sought to secure the right to provide "aid in dying" to patients; (2) court cases, which seek to have state legislation against euthanasia or assisted suicide declared unconstitutional; and (3) the provocative actions of Dr. Jack Kevorkian, a retired Michigan pathologist.

Let us first consider the state referendums. Initiatives to legalize euthanasia were defeated by voters in the State of Washington in 1991 and in California in 1992 by 54% to 46% margins. While these efforts failed, the bad news is that the margin of victory was not great and required the expenditure of significant amounts of money.

More recently, having learned from their failures in Washington and California, the pro-euthanasia forces drafted similar but revised proposals for a referendum in Oregon in order to achieve at least part of their objective and gain the support of a majority of voters. They modified their proposals to exclude lethal injections and to limit the role of physicians to prescribing lethal drugs. This apparently made Measure 16, as it was called, less objectionable to voters. Last November 8, the measure passed by a margin of 51% to 49%, and Oregon became the only state in our nation to decriminalize physician-assisted suicide for terminally ill patients; that is, those who are expected by their doctor to die within six months.

On December 27, 1994, U.S. District Judge Michael Hogan granted a preliminary injunction against implementation of Measure 16. In his opinion, he noted that the "law invokes profound questions of constitutional dimension." He concluded that "surely the first assisted-suicide law in this country deserves a considered, thoughtful constitutional analysis." He also noted the seriousness of the plaintiffs' objections to the

Measure, including, for example, the possibility of misdiagnosis of terminal illness or that physicians and health care workers might be required by the new law to comply with procedures contrary to their religious and moral convictions.

A second set of initiatives has involved challenging state laws that prohibit physician-assisted suicide. Currently, 31 states have statutes banning assisted suicide, and almost all of them have homicide statutes under which it can be prosecuted. In a case in the State of Washington, concluded on May 3, 1994, U.S. District Judge Barbara Rothstein stated that a competent, terminally ill adult *does* have a constitutionally-guaranteed right under the 14th Amendment to commit physician-assisted suicide. This ruling is the *first* judicial decision that alleges a constitutional right to assisted suicide. However, as its critics immediately pointed out, the judge's decision blurred the fundamental moral distinction between *allowing* someone to die and *causing* that person's death. Moreover, Judge Rothstein based her opinion, in large part, on alleged analogies with the U.S. Supreme Court decisions on abortion, especially the 1992 *Planned Parenthood v. Casey*. It comes as no surprise that Judge Rothstein's decision is under appeal.

On December 5, 1994, U.S. District Judge Thomas Griesa in New York came to the opposite conclusion in another case that tried to overturn New York's statute on assisted suicide. The plaintiffs had argued in terms similar to Judge Rothstein's, but Judge Griesa concluded that their attempt to apply Supreme Court abortion decisions on constitutional rights was "too broad." He also held that it is not "unreasonable or irrational for the state to recognize a difference" between "refusing treatment in the case of a terminally ill person and taking a dose of medication which leads to death." The legal battles will continue, and we can expect that, eventually, some cases will appear before the U.S. Supreme Court.

The third kind of initiative in support of assisted suicide is Dr. Jack Kevorkian's public flaunting of a Michigan statute by helping people commit suicide. Last Spring, Dr. Kevorkian was tried under a law that banned assisted suicide, but a Detroit jury, quite surprisingly, found him not guilty even though he had admitted what he had done. The statute's constitutionality has been challenged before the Michigan Supreme Court, and the state legislature is working on another law. Meanwhile, last November, Dr. Kevorkian helped another person commit suicide by supplying her with carbon monoxide gas. This was the 21st death in which he assisted since he began his activities in June, 1990. We can expect that he will vigorously continue his efforts to legalize assisted suicide. Unfortunately, the extensive media coverage about his actions often ignores alternatives available to the elderly and the terminally ill—including, for example, living wills.

The movement to legalize euthanasia or assisted suicide is not confined to the United States. In April of 1990 the Committee on the Environment, Public Health, and Consumer Protection of the European Parliament adopted a motion for a resolution concerning care for the terminally ill. Again, as in some of the proposed U.S. legislation, many of its recommendations were positive and quite acceptable. For example, reflecting widespread concern about the inappropriateness of some aggressive, very burdensome treatments at times of terminal illness, the document acknowledges that "attempts to cure at all costs . . . must be avoided." It also urges that all health care personnel be trained to have a persistently caring attitude toward the dying.

The document further calls for "palliative care" units in all European hospitals to care for those who are terminally ill. Such care seeks to reduce the distressing symptoms of a disease without treating its cause. The goal of this care is to help the patient "fight against pain, discomfort and fear" in the face of incurable illness. Moreover, pointing to the importance of the loving presence of relatives and friends to the dying, the resolution proposes that the treatment of the terminally ill should take place in the familiarity of their home whenever possible.

Unfortunately, the resolution also went far beyond these recommendations. First, in a somewhat subtle manner it sought to redefine the meaning of the human person so that personhood could easily be identified with consciousness. Obviously such a change would have dire consequences for the unconscious, persons with serious mental disorders, and persons with certain disabilities. It is a change that must be resisted.

The document also recommended the use of euthanasia when (1) no cure is available for a terminal illness, (2) palliative care fails, (3) "a fully conscious patient insistently and repeatedly requests an end to an existence which has for him been robbed of all dignity," and (4) "a team of doctors created for that purpose establishes the impossibility of providing further specific care."

In other words, as Archbishop Charles Brand, President of the Commission of the Episcopates of the European Community, has pointed out, the resolution "claims to legitimate acts which terminate life when it is considered to be no longer dignified and human." Such a change not only violates the injunction, "You shall not kill," found in the Decalogue and other foundational religious documents, but also is a radical departure from the entire code of medical ethics as it has been handed on for over two millennia. This code was first expressed in the so-called Hippocratic Oath attributed to an ancient Greek physician. This oath is still used at some medical school graduations. Its second section includes a pledge to use only beneficial treatments and procedures and not to harm or hurt a patient. It includes promises not to break confidentiality, not to engage in sexual relations with patients or to dispense deadly drugs. It specifically says: "I will never give a deadly drug to anybody if asked for it, nor will I make a suggestion to this effect."

In a moment I will speak of the religious and moral issues involved in the rejection of the injunction "you shall not kill." For now, however, I will address the consequences of revising a traditional code of medical ethics which has been widely accepted and respected.

What would happen to the doctor-patient relationship if the proponents of euthanasia or assisted suicide are successful in legalizing these unethical, immoral activities? Would you trust a doctor who is licensed to kill? Would you entrust the life of your elderly mother or father, a seriously ill or disabled child—or your own life—to such a person?

Moreover, what added pressures would patients face? If euthanasia or assisted suicide were legal, might this not influence the decisions of elderly persons, for example, who do not want to be a burden to their families? Would not the poor be especially vulnerable to such pressure? Would they perhaps think that the best thing to do would be to ask their doctors to end their lives before their natural death? Moreover, when we are seriously ill, can we know clearly what we want? Would these truly be free choices?

These are significant, realistic issues which must be addressed. Some would respond by saying that they reflect unnecessary fears, that they are nothing but a "smoke screen" to cover up an attempt to perpetuate an outdated morality. In developing a response to this charge, let us consider what has happened in the Netherlands. The Dutch government has said that only about 200 cases of euthanasia are reported annually. However, according to Catholic News Service, the Remmelink Commission counted 2,340 cases of voluntary euthanasia, 390 cases of assisted suicide, and 1,040 of "life terminating acts without explicit and persistent requests" in 1990 alone! The lives of another 14,000 patients were shortened by pain-killing medication, also *without* their consent.

In other words, the Dutch experiment justifies the concerns I mentioned earlier. There is no convincing evidence that euthanasia or assisted suicide can be regulated and managed. There is a valid reason to be concerned about the impact it would have on the doctor-patient relationship, not to mention the entire code of medical ethics. We may rightly question how safe our most vulnerable persons would be in any society that accepts euthanasia or assisted suicide.

2. Why Is This Movement So Popular?

In the light of information like this one might legitimately question why the euthanasia movement has become so popular. In the United States there are at least three possible explanations.

The first relates to the world of medicine and medical technology. As I noted earlier, for centuries those in the health care professions have had, as an essential aspect of their identity and mission, the responsibility to heal and preserve life. That responsibility has entered a new era with the development of medicines and technologies that have given physicians previously unknown capabilities in this area. We are grateful, indeed, for the great good which these advancements have brought to the human family.

This good, however, has been a mixed blessing. It is fairly easy for technology or medicine to become an end in itself, and for life to be preserved when, in fact, death should be allowed to occur. This possible domination of technology over the proper course of life has left many people fearful of being kept alive in an inhumane fashion. And this fear has led some to say to their loved ones: "Do whatever you must, but do not let me live that way." The fear, then, of the pain and discomfort of a life prolonged inappropriately has led to an erosion of the natural instinct to preserve one's own life.

A second possible explanation is more particular to the United States and its legal system. Although recent years have seen the enactment of legislation that has alleviated many legal problems, a fear remains that sick persons or their families will be prevented from making the necessary medical decisions on their own and that they will have to become embroiled in a contentious legal process.

These two fears—being kept alive needlessly and losing autonomy to the complexity of the legal system—have been exploited by the pro-euthanasia forces in this country. Many people who now favor the legalization of euthanasia or assisted suicide do so, not because they see this as a good in itself, but because they view it as the only avenue available to remedy these fears effectively.

This leads to the third explanation for the spread of pro-euthanasia attitudes. While this reason is present in the United States, it moves far beyond our borders and infects many parts of the world. It pertains to certain assumptions that have dominated, or are beginning to dominate, many of the world's cultures. For our discussion today I will note four such assumptions. In doing so, I am building on the work of Harvard University Professor Arthur J. Dyck.

First, there is a sense of human autonomy which asserts that an individual's life belongs entirely to the individual, and that each person is free to dispose of that life entirely as he or she wishes. Second, in addition to the absence of *external* restraint, there is an understanding of human freedom to make moral choices which says that one must also be free to take one's own life. In other words, there are no *internal* restraints. Third, it is possible to identify times when life simply is not worth living. This can be because of illness or handicaps or even despair. Finally, the true dignity of being human is to be found in the ability to make conscious, rational choices that control life. In the absence of that capacity, human dignity is lessened.

While one might nuance these assumptions, they capture something of the ethos of the euthanasia movement. And to be candid, there is something to be said for these assumptions. For example, they remind us that there are values in addition to the value of physical survival. Also, death is not the worst evil a person can face.

But they also contain great weaknesses. For example, they contain neither limits nor controls. There is no reason to believe they cannot be extended in a fashion similar to that of the Nazi movement to conclusions that would be destructive to the human family in general and, in particular, to those who are the most vulnerable. Moreover, these assumptions self-evidently attack the basic notion of the human person as a member of a human community that is to be characterized by trust and care for one another. In other words, the movement to legalize euthanasia or assisted suicide involves not only decisions at the end of life but also certain assertions or assumptions about the very *nature* of human life.

This means that, if one carefully analyzes the assumptions which would support the legalization of euthanasia, one finds a perspective that challenges the underpinnings of human civilization as we know it. This is why I have chosen this topic for our consideration this evening. As people of faith, we must attend to this threatening force with conviction and fervor. If we remain silent, the course of human history will be significantly altered.

3. A Consistent Ethic of Life

But how can we proceed in a meaningful fashion in a pluralistic society like our own? The obvious answer is that we must find a common ground that will unite us in responding to this challenge, while respecting the religious diversity of our society.

Over the past eleven years I have sought to develop such a common ground within the Catholic tradition through what I have described as a *consistent ethic of life*. I have proposed it as a comprehensive concept and a strategy that will help Catholics and, indeed, all people of good will to influence more effectively the development of public policy on life issues.

The grounding principle for this ethic is found in the Judeo-Christian heritage, which has played such an influential role in the formation of the national ethos of this nation. In this religious tradition, human life is considered *sacred* because God is its origin and its destiny. Consequently, innocent human life must not be directly attacked, threatened, or diminished. Many other people of good will—not of this tradition—also accept the basic premise that human life has a distinctive dignity and meaning or purpose. They, too, argue that, because of the privileged meaning of human life, we have the responsibility for preserving, protecting, and nurturing it.

The second principle underlying the consistent ethic of life is the belief that human life is also *social* in nature. We are not born to live alone, but, rather, to move from the dependency of prenatal life and infancy to the interrelatedness of adulthood. To be human, then, is to be social, and those relationships, structures, and institutions which support us, as individuals and as a community, are an essential aspect of human life.

If one accepts these two principles about human life, then one may argue that two precepts or obligations necessarily flow from them. First, as individuals and as a society, we have the positive obligation to protect and nurture life. Second, we have a negative obligation not to destroy or injure human life directly, especially the life of the innocent and the vulnerable.

These principles and the resulting precepts have served as the foundation for much of what is known as the Anglo-Saxon legal tradition. They are the context for laws which oppose abortion, murder, and euthanasia or assisted suicide. This movement from religious insight to public policy is an important one. In the common law tradition these laws have been maintained, not because of religious insight, but because it is recognized that they pertain to the *common good* of society. In other words, the commonweal of public life and order would be destroyed if innocent human life could be directly attacked. In more recent years this same insight regarding the fundamental dignity of the human person has been given international recognition in the Universal Declaration of Human Rights.

I have addressed the need for a consistent ethic of life because new technological challenges confront us along the whole spectrum of life from conception to natural death. This creates the need for a consistent ethic, for the spectrum cuts across such life-threatening issues as abortion, capital punishment, modern warfare, and the care of the terminally ill. Admittedly, these are all *distinct,* complex problems which deserve individual treatment. Each requires its own moral analysis. No single answer or solution applies to all. At any given time, because of the circumstances, one may demand more attention than another. *But they are linked!*

Moreover, life-*threatening* issues are also linked with life-*diminishing* issues such as racism, sexism, pornography, prostitution, and child abuse. Wherever human life is considered "cheap" and easily exploited or wasted, respect for life dwindles and, eventually, every human life is in jeopardy.

The concept of a consistent ethic of life is challenging. It requires people to broaden, substantively and creatively, their way of thinking, their attitudes, their response to life issues. Many are not accustomed to thinking about all the life-threatening and life-diminishing issues in such an interrelated way. As a result, they remain somewhat selective in their response. Some, for example, are very committed in their efforts to eradicate the evil of abortion in this nation, but neglect issues of poverty. Others work very hard to alleviate poverty, but neglect the basic right to life of unborn children.

Given this broad range of challenging life issues, we desperately need a societal *attitude* or climate that will sustain a consistent defense and promotion of life. In other words, it is not enough merely to assert an ethical principle like the consistent ethic of life. It must also be implemented and when it is, it necessarily impacts all areas of human life. It responds to all the moments, places, or conditions which either threaten the sanctity of life or cultivate an attitude of disrespect for it. A consistent ethic is based on the need to ensure that the sacredness of every human life, which is the ultimate source of human dignity, is defended and fostered from the genetic laboratory to the cancer ward, from the ghetto to the prison.

The movement from moral analysis to public policy choices is a complex process in a pluralistic society like the United States. There is a legitimate secularity of the political process. But there is also a legitimate role for religious and moral discourse in our nation's life because nearly every important social issue has a moral or ethical dimension. Moreover, this ethical dimension usually does not exist apart from complex empirical judgments where honest disagreement may exist even among those who agree on the principles involved.

In the legal tradition of our country, however, it is not the function of civil law to enjoin or prohibit *everything* that moral principles enjoin or prohibit. So when dealing with law or public policy we must ask, in addition to the moral or ethical implications, whether the requirements of public order and the common good are serious enough to take precedence over the claims of freedom. Achieving a consensus on what constitutes a matter which is both moral or ethical and essential for public order and the common good is not easy. But we have been able to do it—by a process of debate, decision-making, then a review of our decisions and their impact on human lives, especially the most vulnerable.

My efforts to articulate the need for a consistent ethic of life have helped many people, both Catholic and non-Catholic, see the need for addressing in a consistent way a full range of life issues from conception to natural death. Moreover, I believe that human life has a meaning and a purpose that affirm the integrity and inherent value of body and spirit, even in the midst of suffering. I also affirm that all human persons need and desire to be able to trust the community in which they abide. And I am convinced that *individual* choices influence the moral tone and character of the *community* and, indeed, the entire human family.

That is why I am opposed to the legalization of euthanasia. It compromises the fundamental dignity of the human person in its inordinate exaltation of rational consciousness and in its challenge to the belief that there is significance to human suffering. It does inconceivable violence to the trust that should exist between doctor and patient—and, indeed, among all human persons. And it naively pretends that individual human choices are isolated moments which have no impact on the lives and well-being of others. Both my faith and experience tell me otherwise!

Letter to the Supreme Court[23]

November 7, 1996

I am at the end of my earthly life. There is much that I have contemplated these last few months of my illness, but as one who is dying I have especially come to appreciate the gift of life. I know from my own experience that patients often face difficult and deeply personal decisions about their care. However, I also know that even a person who decides to forgo treatment does not necessarily choose death. Rather, he chooses life without the burden of disproportionate medical intervention.

In this case the court faces one of the most important issues of our times. Physician-assisted suicide is decidedly a public matter. It is not simply a decision made beween patient and physician. Because life affects every person, it is of primary public concern.

I have often remarked that I admire the writings of the late Father John Courtney Murray, who argued that an issue was related to public policy if it affected the public order of society. And public order, in turn, encompassed three goods, public peace, the essential protection of human rights and commonly accepted standards of moral behavior in a community.

Our legal and ethical tradition has held consistently that suicide, assisted suicide and euthanasia are wrong because they involve a direct attack on innocent human life. And it is a matter of public policy because it involves a violation of a fundamental human good.

There can be no such thing as a "right to assisted suicide," because there can be no legal and moral order which tolerates the killing of innocent human life, even if the agent of death is self-administered. Creating a new "right" to assisted suicide will endanger society and send a false signal that a less-than-"perfect" life is not worth living.

Physician-assisted suicide also directly affects the physician-patient relationship and, through that, the wider role of physicians in our society. As has been noted by others, it introduces a deep ambiguity into the very definition of medical care if care comes to involve killing. Beyond the physician, a move to assisted suicide, and perhaps beyond that to euthanasia, creates social ambiguity about the law. In civilized society the law exists to protect life. When it begins to legitimate the taking of life as a policy, one has a right to ask what lies ahead for our life together as a society.

In order to protect patients from abuse and to protect society from a dangerous erosion in its commitment to preserving human life, I urge the court not to create any right to assisted suicide.

Managing Managed Care

International Association of Catholic Medical Schools
Loyola University of Chicago
May 13, 1996

Introduction

It is an honor to be with this distinguished international assembly of medical educators this morning. I trust that those of you who are not from this country will indulge me as I share some reflections on the transformation of the United States' health care system. Although these reflections are couched in the specifics of our experience, many of the issues involved are universal and are the subject of debate in other countries as well.

The next class of Catholic medical school graduates will begin their careers in the coming millennium. We are inclined to think of such chronological watersheds as defining epochal shifts in human behavior and institutions. In the remaining years of the 20th century we are likely to be barraged with predictions and prophecies of what the new century, and the millennium it ushers in, will bring.

In the field of health care, however, history has had a head start. The new epoch has not waited for the new millennium; it is already well under way. Among the significant forces for 21st century health care that have defined themselves in the past decade are the following: the explosion of genetic information that brings new hope and new ethical challenges seemingly each week; the aging of our society and of the industrialized world; and the revolution in information that expands our horizons and jeopardizes our privacy.

This morning, I will address the phenomenon that will inform the organization and delivery of health care in the next century. You do not have to be a futurist or a prophet to know that this is the phenomenon known as *managed care*. In the United States, with more than half of our insured population in some form of managed care, we have already entered the era of managed care. Our challenge for the coming years is in *managing* managed care to ensure that it contributes to the purposes of health care for each person and the common good.

I come to this discussion as a pastor, a bishop, a leader of our National Conference of Catholic Bishops, and a member of the Board of the Catholic Health Association of the United States. In these capacities I have, with my colleagues, wrestled with the issues raised by managed care and sought to develop responses compatible with our Catholic heritage and health care mission. I have pursued this within the context of the consistent ethic of life which I have articulated over the past twelve years.

The purpose of the consistent life ethic is to provide a moral framework for analysis and motivation for action on a wide range of human life-issues with important ethical dimensions. The foundation for this framework is a deep conviction about the nature of human life, namely, that human life is sacred, which means that all human life has an inalienable dignity that must be protected and respected from conception to death. It is from this vantage point that we consider the nature and value of managed care.

In its relatively brief history, managed care has become many things to many people:

- To some federal policy-makers, it is a way to assure the solvency of the Medicare program and to stretch Medicaid dollars further.
- To teaching hospitals and medical schools, it is a danger to broad-based support for medical research and education.
- To some patients, it is the loss of choice of a provider; to other patients, it is a greater array of benefits, including preventive services.
- To some ethicists, it is a back-door rationing scheme; to others, it is a prudent use of scarce social resources.

Managed care appears to be so many different things, in part, because it is a broad term that covers many different health care financing and delivery arrangements. In this discussion, I use the term "managed care" to describe an insurance or delivery mechanism that involves one or more of the following elements:

- limiting the number of providers serving a covered population, either through direct ownership or employment, or through selective contracting or through some combination of these elements;

- adherence by providers to utilization management controls;
- incentives for patients to use only the providers designated by the managed care plan;
- some degree of financial risk for providers, ranging from HMOs that assume full risk for the cost of care to contractual arrangements under which carriers and providers share risk.

The diversity of views on managed care stems in part from the great variety of ways in which the elements of managed care are applied. It is also true, however, that part of the controversy about managed care results from its impact on the health care system. Many of the traditional health care relationships—between doctors and patients, between insurers and doctors, between hospitals and doctors, between patients and insurers, to name a few—are being dramatically affected by the transition to managed care. In some cases, entirely new entities are being created that replace or restructure existing relationships.

In these times of radical change in the U.S. health care system, we should not be surprised that there are many opinions and many public policy issues. Health care is intensely personal. Each of us and our family members has a direct, personal stake in the cost, availability, and quality of health care. In addition, since health care in this nation is a more than $1 trillion enterprise, the financial stakes for government, insurers, employers, hospitals, physicians, and others are also great, as managed care produces new winners and losers in the marketplace.

We must remember, however, that no system of health care is an end in itself. We must examine managed care in terms of the nature of health and purpose of health care and how it advances or detracts from those purposes. We may also look at managed care in historical terms: Has it brought improvements over the methods of financing and delivery it is replacing? Are there things of value that are being lost?

Health Care Values

What are the principles and values of health care against which managed care should be measured? The goal of health care is healing. To heal is to restore wholeness, "to make whole that which is impaired or less than whole." Achieving wholeness requires attention not only to the physical condition of the patient, but also to his or her spiritual and social well-being. Further, health care is focused not only on curing illness, but also on preventing it and building "wellness." Health care is not focused solely on the patient, but also attends to the overall health of the community. No person can be completely well if his or her community is unhealthy, and a community's health is dependent on that of its members. To fulfill these purposes, a health care system must embody the following values:

- Health care must be a service. Care of those who are ill and dying is an important measure of the moral character of a society. Health care is an essential social good, a service to persons in need; it cannot be a mere commodity exchanged for profit, access to which depends on financial resources.
- Each person's human dignity must be preserved. Because health care is critical to human dignity, all persons have a right to basic, comprehensive health care of the highest quality.
- The common good must be served. Dignity is realized only in association with others. Health care must serve the good of the nation and the community—as well as the individual.
- The needs of the poor must have special priority. The wealthy and well must not ignore their obligation to help care for the poor and the sick. The health fate of the poor should be tied to that of the average U.S. citizen.
- There must be responsible stewardship of resources. Our resources are not unlimited and must be managed wisely. The health care system must use economic discipline to hold health care spending within realistic limits.
- Health care should be provided at appropriate levels of organization. It should respect local diversity, preserve pluralism in delivery, protect a range of choice and preserve the relationship between physician and patient.

In considering managed care and its significance for achieving the purposes and values of health care, it is important to recognize the context from which managed care springs. Many of the same forces driving the growth of managed care are also propelling changes in other areas of society. In the private sector, global competition has led companies to seek efficiencies through consolidations, downsizings, and reducing the cost of benefits. In the public sector, continuing federal deficits and resistance to tax increases have led to constraints on government expenditures at all levels for all purposes.

The Traditional System

Health care has not been immune from the impact of these forces. Indeed, it is regarded by many as a major contributor to excessive costs and inefficiencies of both the public and private sectors. So, the strengths and weaknesses of the health care system that existed before managed care are also part of the context of managed care. Before turning to a consideration of managed care, I will briefly describe the health care system that it appears to be on its way to replacing.

In this discussion I shall refer to managed care's predecessor as the "traditional" system, although in many respects that system has become prevalent only in the post-World War II years. In its full blossoming, between 1965 and 1985, the traditional system was characterized

- by a proliferation of clinically and economically independent health care providers, such as doctors and hospitals;
- by employment-based health insurance for a majority, but by no means all, of the non-aged, non-poor population;
- by fee-for-service payment for medical services by the individual, employer, private insurance carrier or government program;
- by a growing government presence both as an insurer for selected populations and as a funder of health care research and education; and
- by health care institutions, particularly hospitals, and insurers that were predominantly locally based and not-for-profit.

Looking at the strengths and weaknesses of traditional health care in terms of the health care values I outlined earlier, we see a mixed picture. For those with adequate insurance or sufficient personal resources, traditional health care's strengths include maximizing the choice of providers for patients, and clinical freedom for physicians. Subject to broad categories of insurance coverage and general definitions of medical necessity, a patient and a physician had relatively few limitations on treatment options.

The traditional system also was characterized by pluralism in the delivery system and by a commitment to the highest quality medicine through public and private support for research and education. The view of health care as a service—as opposed to a commodity—was widespread among physicians and not-for-profit hospitals that provided charity care. Paradoxically, however, the advent of government health care programs may have eroded the private sector's commitment to health care as a service.

The traditional system's weaknesses include the absence of a right to health care for all and the lack of a strong commitment to public health. Although problems were mitigated by community-rated health insurance plans and Medicaid, health care for the poor remained haphazard. The traditional system contributed little toward the responsible stewardship of resources. Indeed, for physicians and other providers, the traditional system offered financial incentives to provide unneeded services and no reason for insured patients not to seek additional care, regardless of its likelihood for success. It may be argued that the relentlessly rising costs of traditional care acted as a brake on expanding health care services to the poor and the elderly under existing programs as well as efforts to achieve universal coverage as a matter of right.

Managed Care

Managed care is, in part, a response to the perceived problems of traditional health care. We are limited in assessing its strengths and weaknesses relative to our fundamental health care values because of its relative newness, its many forms, and its still-evolving nature. A key attraction of managed care is that it offers a vehicle for enhancing the value of stewardship. By emphasizing the efficient use of health care resources, managed care appears to have contributed to the recent moderation in health care cost increases for employers and governments. By extension, managed care offers the possibility, through containing costs, of broadening access to health care through stretching government budgets and encouraging more employers to offer coverage to their employees.

Many types of managed care plans, because they are financially responsible for all the health care a person may use, have a strong incentive to provide preventive health care and careful management of chronic conditions to avoid costly complications. At the same time, however, these incentives can encourage plans to try to limit their enrollment to healthier populations as a "preventive" technique. A final and important strength of many managed care plans is the promotion of quality by identifying, disseminating, and reinforcing the most effective medical practices to their physicians and other providers.

As I have noted, in some aspects, the features of managed care that promote certain health care values may threaten others. Financial incentives to conserve resources can lead to providing too few services even as the traditional system can lead to the provision of too many services. Implicit pressures—such as the linking of physician compensation to cost targets—or explicit practice guidelines can result in limitations on access to needed services. Managed care promotes the consolidation of health care services—the grouping of doctors, hospitals, and other providers through employment or contracting into networks. This offers economies of scale that contain costs, but also threaten the continued independence of health care institutions that contribute to pluralism in our system. I speak here of Catholic and other religiously affiliated or charitable institutions whose missions are explicitly and intimately bound to the poor and the vulnerable. Also, because managed care typically contributes less support for research and medical education than the traditional system, we must examine the needs of these programs, as well as appropriate funding mechanisms.

As I have expressed on other occasions, there can be little doubt that there are good reasons to change our health care system, among them the need to improve the stewardship of our resources. The rapid growth of managed care, however, has heightened concerns that the economics of health care may unduly predominate over other fundamental health care values. Economics have always played a role in health care, but managed care systems require exceptionally large infusions of capital, primarily to fund the data bases and computer systems needed to monitor care and cut costs, and to fund the creation of networks through the purchase of physician practices. The need for such capital has led an increasing number of not-for-profit hospitals to convert to for-profit status or to enter into joint ventures with for-profit hospital companies. And, while the need to produce a return to stockholders may spur continuous efforts to improve efficiency, it also raises the concern that managed care plans may be tempted to achieve efficiencies by restricting needed care.

Rationing

Many of the concerns about managed care are related—directly or indirectly—to this fear: namely, that the economic imperatives of managed care will result in the inappropriate rationing of health care services. If we accept, as we must, that our resources are finite, then we must address this issue openly and clearly. The very concept of rationing is explosive. I prefer the concept of "stewardship." How do we best protect human life and enhance human dignity in a situation of limited health resources?

If we define rationing as the withholding of potentially beneficial health care services because policies and practices establish limits on the resources available for health care, rationing becomes an issue of balance between the individual and the community, both of which have acknowledged needs. Under this definition, we do not prejudge the issue of whether a specific proposal or method of rationing is good or evil; we leave open the possibility that withholding care may be justified by limits on resources.

This is not an abstract discussion. Rationing health care is a regular, if unacknowledged, feature of both our traditional health care system and of our system as modified by managed care. As a nation, we ration health care by choosing not to adopt a system of universal health care coverage. As a result, nearly 40 million are uninsured and some 50 million more are underinsured. Government programs, such as Medicare and Medicaid, ration access to care on the basis of age, income, and family composition. Private health care is rationed by a person's or an employer's ability and willingness to pay. It is also rationed through insurance marketing techniques such as medical underwriting, pre-existing condition exclusion, and red-lining.

In my own life, as a person diagnosed with pancreatic cancer, I could have been denied treatment on several different grounds:

- my age—if I had been under 65 (the Medicare qualifying age) and uninsured;
- the expected outcome for persons of my age and health; or
- lack of coverage by my health plan for a specific procedure.

I also could have been discouraged, directly or indirectly, from seeking treatment if my physician had incentives to inform me of only certain treatments or incentives to provide needed treatments for my condition in a facility far from my home and loved ones. In my case, however, I was well-insured through a combination of private coverage paid by my diocese and Medicare that allowed me and my physicians maximum flexibility in selecting a treatment regimen.

Two years ago, I called for national health reform that assured universal coverage for all Americans, that is, to end the rationing of access to health care through denial of insurance. In that context, I pointed out that we would have to undertake a broad-based and inclusive consideration of how to allocate and share our limited health care dollars. It is proper, based on a moral consensus, for society to establish limits on what it can reasonably provide in one area of the commonweal so that it can address other legitimate responsibilities. Although the national debate over universal access unfortunately has been stilled for the present, the Catholic Health Association has addressed the ethics of rationing and offered some moral criteria.

These criteria demand that any acceptable rationing plan must meet a demonstrable need, be oriented to the common good, result from an open and participatory process, apply to all, give priority to disadvantaged persons, be free of wrongful discrimination, and be monitored in its social effects. Although these criteria were conceived in the context of developing a universal health plan, most of them are still as appropriate to the rationing decisions of private health plans as they are to public programs and should be applied to managed care in both sectors.

For example, an employer purchasing a health care plan should look not only at price, but also at the policies of any plan that may limit needed care. The employer is obligated to consider whether its resources or those of its employees are so limited as to justify a health plan that relies on rationing. The employer must also be sure that access to any health plan offered is equitable. When employers contribute a greater share of the premium cost for employees earning lower wages, they reduce the potential for rationing based on ability to pay.

Likewise, some states may have a genuine problem raising tax money for their Medicaid programs. But others have simply decided, for political expedience, to maximize, that is, not to diminish some of their citizens' disposable incomes, regardless of the unmet health care needs among their poorer citizens. This is irresponsible. Health care rationing in this context is unfair.

As I have pointed out, such rationing is not unique to managed care. Indeed, it has been a staple in the traditional system. Under that system, however, rationing although reprehensible, is relatively visible. Managed care may require greater scrutiny to ensure that rationing decisions are transparent to patients and the public.

Managing Managed Care

In terms of the health care values we uphold—human dignity, stewardship, the common good—managed care offers both *promise* and *peril*. By restraining costs, it offers the possibility of including more persons under public and private insurance. By explicitly addressing the appropriateness of care through practice guidelines and other means, it offers the possibility of improving the quality of health care and eliminating unnecessary care. By focusing on prevention, it offers the possibility of avoiding or mitigating many serious and disabling conditions.

As I have noted, however, the market forces and economic disciplines that are the engines of managed care can be socially insensitive and ethically blind. In managing managed care we must find ways to encourage and sustain its benefits and to constrain those tendencies which, if left unattended, could undermine important health care values.

Because managed care is not a single phenomenon, but, rather, a variety of organizations, practices, and techniques that share almost as many differences as commonalities, its deficiencies, present and potential, defy sweeping diagnosis and prescription. At the same time, it is clear that managed care raises issues that go right to the social and ethical core of our health care values. As managed care asserts itself as the health care paradigm for the next century, we are obligated to confront these issues and shape its development. I have organized my own reflections on managed care around three groupings of issues: (1) those dealing with the *common good*; (2) those affecting the *quality* of health care; and, finally, (3) issues relating to *stewardship* and *rationing*.

First, I will address the *common good,* the social dimension of managed care. The paramount health care issue of our time is the affront to human dignity that is occasioned by the lack of universal insurance coverage for even basic care. In addition to the fear, insecurity, and inadequate health care that afflict individuals, the existence of rural and inner city hospitals that care for the uninsured is threatened by competitive managed care. While in theory managed care should help free up resources to cover such persons, it is not clear, despite some innovative state experiments, that managed care savings from public programs will be recycled to expand coverage. On the private side, it is a troubling fact that, despite several years of moderation in the growth of employer health care costs, which many attribute in large part to the growth of managed care, the number of persons covered by employer insurance has declined, not increased. It is not enough to argue that, without managed care, more persons would lose their insurance. We must use the benefits of managed care to help achieve the broadest possible coverage of our population.

In this regard, we must also develop mechanisms to provide appropriate support for education and research from all participants in the health care system. In general, managed care plans avoid sending patients to hospitals and other institutions with primary responsibility for training health care professionals and conducting medical research—activities that provide broad public benefits. At the same time, our teaching priorities must be adjusted to produce an appropriate number and balance of specialists and primary care providers. Research must also give greater emphasis to public health issues and behavioral problems.

The last social issue I will comment on is not peculiar to managed care, but is one that could be compounded by the competitive environment in which managed care operates. We must develop and adopt methods to compensate health plans that enroll disproportionate numbers of sick people at the expense of plans that enroll disproportionate numbers of healthy people. If we do not, we will witness a morally repugnant system in which plans will compete to avoid caring for the sick, to avoid a central purpose of health care altogether. These methods, known as "risk adjustment," reduce incentives for managed care plans to compete based on enrolling only healthier populations.

I turn now to a set of issues relating to the *quality* of care. Responsible decisions about managing health care depend on good data regarding health outcomes. While increasing attention has been given to this issue by both public and private agencies, much remains to be done. We should take an expanded view of outcomes, going beyond death and illness rates to include functional outcomes, the quality of life from the patient's perspective, and the satisfaction of both patient and provider. Doctors and hospitals should be leaders in the effort to develop and put into use measures of successful care.

These measures should be available to all. Managed care networks should issue annual report cards to the public on their enrollees' demographic characteristics, their health status, the number and kinds of services rendered, and the outcomes of these services. Such report cards will help families choose plans more wisely and will provide the public with the information needed to manage managed care.

Ultimately, quality health care is more than the sum of statistical outcomes. The use of practice guidelines should be expanded to include a strong patient role in the decision process. Patient education and empowerment programs have demonstrated better outcomes and lower costs when patients are fully informed and active participants. Most importantly, the patient's active involvement in medical decisions is a critical ingredient in the preservation of human dignity.

Finally, let us consider the issues of *stewardship* and *rationing*. As I mentioned a moment ago, there remains the fundamental challenge of universally assuring access to health care. Until this is achieved, some of the rationing implications of managed care pose moral problems. The crux of this problem is that, while universal access creates a floor of benefits, rationing creates a ceiling. We find ourselves moving toward a morally untenable situation in which we are building health care ceilings without floors—a regime in which there will be no limits on how little care one might receive, only on how much.

In the absence of universal coverage, however, we must focus on how health care ceilings are built. For instance, the adoption of practice protocols and other explicit care-determining policies by managed care plans should include a formal role for physicians participating in the plan, as medical staffs at most hospitals participate in decisions with clinical implications. Plan enrollees should also be consulted and there should be provision for public oversight.

Even with such precautions, there remains the potential that economic incentives for doctors and other providers in managed care plans may lead to *ad hoc* rationing decisions that are designed to protect income, not the patient. Some reward for physicians' efforts to make care more economical is appropriate, but financial incentives to physicians to constrain care should be limited to avoid the potential for less than optimal care. One approach to this problem is contained in recent federal regulations that require Medicare HMOs to limit the financial risk of participating physicians to specified levels. This is intended to reduce possible conflicts between a physician's pocketbook and the patient's needs. In general, financial incentives should cover a group of doctors so that the focus is on promoting efficient practice patterns for all patients, not on rewarding individual physicians for denying care to individual patients.

Information on managed care plans' policies that limit care and on physician financial incentives should be made available to all enrollees. Physicians must be free to discuss these issues directly with patients without fear of penalty. When controversies arise about the appropriateness of care, there must be clear guidelines for appeal within a plan, and physicians should have the explicit role of advocacy on behalf of their patients. These concerns go to the trust that must be at the heart of the doctor-patient relationship, a trust that in many ways is being challenged today and which we must work to strengthen, as I indicated in a recent address to the House of Delegates of the American Medical Association.

Conclusion

Managing managed care must involve both the public and private sectors, and there are many initiatives toward this end currently under way by individual health care systems and others. Large employer and employee coalitions can play an important role by demanding outcomes-based quality measures from plans that seek their business. Health care provider organizations, such as the American Medical Association, the National Committee for Quality Assurance, and the Joint Commission on the

Accreditation of Hospitals and Other Health Care Organizations, also have a critical role to play in helping to ensure that managed care contributes to the values of human dignity and social good.

The Catholic Health Association, in its proposal for health care reform, entitled "Setting Relationships Right," has addressed many of these issues. And Catholic health providers, such as the several Mercy Health Systems, have developed explicit ethical guidelines for managed care contract negotiations.

By encouraging prudent use of our resources, managed care can help us achieve a broader and, ultimately, universal health care coverage. It can help improve quality standards and reduce unnecessary and dangerous medical care. It can promote preventive care and wellness. It can nurture comprehensive primary care relationships between patients and physicians.

Like most human endeavors, however, managed care contains within it the potential for creating as many problems as it solves. Without vigilance and thoughtful, constructive engagement, we could find that instead of expanding coverage, managed care might function primarily as an instrument to ensure that those who now enjoy health care coverage continue to do so. This is important—we do not wish to see an erosion of coverage—but it is not enough. We could find that new, unacceptable means of rationing are added to those that already exist. We could find that economic goals supplant health goals. We could find that the trust that is so essential to the doctor-patient relationship might be undermined by financial incentives.

As we approach the new century, changes in the health care system will continue to accelerate. By evaluating and responding to those changes in terms of our consistent life ethic and our health care values, we have the opportunity and the obligation to manage managed care so that it advances the goals of human dignity and the common good.

The Catholic Moral Vision in the United States

Georgetown University
September 9, 1996

Let me begin by expressing my appreciation to Georgetown University, and particularly to Father Leo O'Donovan, for inviting me to return here to reflect upon the public life and witness of the Catholic Church in the context of U.S. society and culture. Each time I have come to Georgetown, it has been in a presidential election year, but I regard that as a secondary consideration. The Church must reflect continuously on its public witness. That witness is rooted in religious and moral convictions, so the reflection must be theological in its foundation and then related to the issues of policy that shape the life of our society.

This afternoon, I seek to provide a "broad" interpretation of the Church's public witness. It will be broad in two senses: First, I will address three large areas of intersection between the Catholic moral vision and U.S. society: (1) religion and politics, (2) economic choices and social justice, and (3) the sanctity of life and U.S. culture. Second, in each area— politics, economics, and culture—I propose to look not only at how Catholic teaching speaks to American society, but how these issues should be reflected upon in the internal life of the Church itself.

Building upon the premise that theological principles should ground our thinking about the Church's public life, I will rely principally upon a major teaching document for each area of my address, using Vatican II's *Declaration on Religious Liberty* for religion and politics, the U.S. Catholic bishops' pastoral letter on the economy (*Economic Justice for All*) for justice and the economy, and Pope John Paul II's *The Gospel of Life* to address life and culture.

I. Religion and Politics: The American Style

The relationship of religion and politics is as old as the U.S. constitutional tradition. The nation was founded in great part by those who had experienced religious discrimination or who were wary of any close connection of religion and politics. Religious pluralism has been for this nation both a factual condition and a constitutionally protected characteristic of the society almost from its inception. Precisely because of its centrality to the U.S. political tradition, the issue of religion and politics requires constant intellectual attention. Commentators have often noted an apparent paradox: Religion is kept strictly separate from the institution of the state, yet the U.S. public overwhelmingly thinks of itself as a religious people, with a very high percentage consistently affirming their religious convictions. The paradox is apparent because an argument can be made that careful distinctions between religion and politics may be in fact our source of religious vitality. I suggest we think of the role of religion in our society in terms of three questions: church and state, church and civil society and, finally, religion and politics.

The church–state question is the central structural element in understanding the role of religion in U.S. society. For all its centrality, however, it is actually a quite limited issue. It is best, I think, to try to keep it both limited in its significance and clear in its content. The church–state relationship governs how the institution of the state will relate to religiously-based institutions in our society. To discuss, debate, or analyze church and state is not at all to engage the full range of religious conviction, commitment, and engagement in our society. The church–state relationship is narrow, juridical, and institutional in character. It is governed by the First Amendment to the U.S. Constitution, and essentially affirms that religious communities should expect neither special assistance from the state nor any discrimination in the exercise of their civil and religious activity in society. This description of the meaning of the First Amendment does not attempt to exegete the court decisions that address specific dimensions of the law. It is, rather, a political interpretation of this standard element of our constitutional life. From the perspective of Catholic teaching, embodied in the *Declaration on Religious Liberty*, the political meaning of the First Amendment is good law. It protects what the Second Vatican Council and Pope Paul VI asserted was the basic requirement of church–state relations in any culture: the freedom of the Church. Keeping secular and religious institutions distinct in purpose and function, in fact, creates space for the Church to teach, preach, and serve. Having the freedom to function guaranteed by law allows the Church—and any religious community in this society—to define its ministry, pursue its religious and civil objectives, and demonstrate the transforming power of faith, love, and grace in society.

It is precisely when the church–state relations are clearly defined in law, that the second dimension of the role of religion in society becomes centrally important: the relationships, networks, institutions, and associations that lie "beyond the state," that is, they are neither created by the state nor are they controlled by the state. The concept of civil society is captured in the distinction between state and society that is pivotal in the Western liberal tradition of politics and that both Jacques Maritain and John Courtney Murray used in building the case within Catholicism for the right of religious liberty.

Both external and internal events in the United States have refocused scholarly attention and policy debates about the role and function of civil society. The collapse of communism in Central Europe and the former Soviet Union has yielded proposals from the West on how "to shrink" the state and build the fabric of civil society. At the same time, troubling trends in the United States on issues as diverse as family life, education, citizen participation, and general standards of civility have concentrated attention on the quality and character of our own civil society. It is in the fabric of civil society that religious communities and institutions flourish. In terms of the U.S. political tradition, it is crucially important to stress that the logic of church–state relations, which lays stress on legitimate separation of secular and sacral institutions, should not govern the logic of civil society. The logic of this relationship is **engagement,** not separation. In other words, to endorse a properly secular state, which has no established ties to any religious institution, does not imply or mean that we should support a secularized society, one in which religion is reduced to a purely private role.

Both Catholic social theory and U.S. constitutional principles support a substantive role and place for religion in the fabric of our society and culture. The state will not and should not be the agent for advancing a substantive conception of religious values and principles in the life of the nation, but the state should not be hostile to the enterprise. Precisely because of the pervasive role of religious convictions among the citizens of our society, there is a legitimate place in our national life for these convictions to find expression.

Civil society is a sphere of freedom; it provides political and legal space for a multiplicity of actors and institutions to help form and shape the fabric of our national life and culture. In this sphere of freedom, religious institutions can exercise the full range of their ministries of teaching and service. Religious witness will only be as effective and as persuasive as the religious communities render it through the lives and work of their leaders and members. This is the meaning of being "free to function." We can demand this right; then we must meet our responsibilities.

While the constitutional framework that generates our place in civil society is clear enough, it is also clear that one finds in the debate about civil society today some voices that are less than comfortable with a vigorous role for religious institutions in our public life and policy debates. This may in part be due to the way some religious witness is undertaken. But it is also the case that some versions of civil society are advanced, which carry the logic of separation to the point where the public life of our society would lose its religious content.

If this happened, I submit, we would be a poorer culture and society. There is clearly no place for religious coercion or proselytization in our public life, but there is a broad area in which religious ideas and institutions can contribute to issues as diverse as strengthening the family, humanizing the drive of economic competition, and defining our responsibilities as a nation in a very changed world.

To those who are skeptical or simply opposed to a public role for religion, and to the community of believers upon whom lies the responsibility for religious witness, I submit there are three ways in which religious traditions can enrich civil society. The first is through religious vision and discourse. The Hebrew scriptures tell us that, where there is no vision, people perish. A constant responsibility of religious communities is to enrich our public vision through the resources of ideas, values, principles, and images that are the core of any great tradition.

In my own tradition, I have tried to take the theme of the sacredness of the human person and develop its implications through "A Consistent Ethic" of life. The ideas supporting the consistent ethic have been cultivated in the Catholic moral tradition for centuries. But the convergence of forces arising from contemporary society to threaten human life and sacredness creates a new context in which the ancient themes of an ethic of stewardship of life take on new relevance. Essentially, I have argued, as I will this afternoon, that we must systematically address a series of threats to life by building within civil society a shared vision of what human sacredness demands and how we install binding principles of restraint and respect in our personal codes of conduct and in our public policies.

The theme of "A Consistent Ethic" is only one way in which a religious tradition can enrich our public dialogue. I realize that part of the apprehension of some citizens, scholars, and analysts is that religious convictions that are not universally shared will be thrust into our policy debates. I understand the concern, and I will return to it in this address, but here I simply want to establish the point that a policy of **excluding** religious vision, discourse, and insights from our search for coherent, just, viable public policies is a price too high to pay. Without vision, people perish; we need all the resources we can muster today in developing an adequate vision for our society.

But religion is not exhausted by ideas and vision alone. A second crucial contribution it can make to civil society is through the ministry and work of religious institutions of education, health care, family service, and direct outreach to the poorest parts of our society. The web of religious institutions is a pervasive aspect of our social support system. I believe it is the time to think intensively about how a more extensive public-private pattern of collaboration could serve to extend the range of effectiveness of these institutions and at the same time use scarce public resources more efficiently in support of human needs.

Thirdly, perhaps the most effective, long-term contribution that religious communities make to civil society is the kind of citizens who are shaped, often decisively, by participation in a religious tradition. In Christian terms this is the link between discipleship and citizenship. Recent research, reflected in the work of Robert Putnam at Harvard University, as well as that of John Coleman and David Hollenbach in the Catholic community, point to the way in which religious affiliation has a decisive impact on the kind of civic engagement of individuals, particularly engagement in the service of others.

In summary, my argument thus far has been in support of clear distinctions between church and state, in opposition to any exclusion of religion from civil society, and in advocacy of a broad, deep, activist role for religious institutions in shaping our public life.

There is a final piece of this argument, this one directed to the religious communities rather than civil society: the theme of religion and politics. My point here is that a proper understanding of both the logic of **separation** (church and state) and the logic of **engagement** (church and civil society) locates the church in the proper place for public witness. **How** religion engages the political order is a question of style, and style here carries major importance. Style refers to the way religious communities speak to the political process, and style also refers to the manner in which we engage others in debate and discussion. One reason why some have apprehension about religious involvement in public life is the style sometimes employed by religious institutions or communities. My proposal, therefore, is that effective religious witness depends, in part, on our style of participation. Engagement in civil society must be characterized by commitment and civility; witness must be a blend of advocacy and restraint. I am hardly pressing for a timid or feeble religious voice! My concern, rather, is to establish from *within* religious communities standards of participation that will shape our public witness.

Allow me to use two examples. First, while I know there is a healthy debate on this topic among scholars, I am inclined to the view that our style of arguing a social position ought to distinguish among how we speak within the church, how we participate in civil society, and how we address the state on law and policy. Within the church, the full range of biblical, theological themes that structure our belief should be used. Within civil society, I also think that explicit appeal to religious warrants and imperatives is both legitimate and needed if we are to address some of the profoundly human themes that are at the heart of our policy debates. But when we address the state, I believe we should be ascetic in our use of explicitly religious appeals. Here we seek to shape law and policy that will obligate all in society. At this point we accept the responsibility of making our religiously grounded convictions intelligible to those who do not share the faith that yields these convictions.

Secondly, our style of religious witness should constantly be a testimony to the theological virtue of charity, which, in turn, produces the civic virtue of civility. Vigorous pursuit of our deepest convictions—even those involving life and death—should not involve questioning the motives of others, or their character. We should vigorously oppose conclusions we find unwise or immoral; we should vigorously pursue objectives that are essential for human life and dignity. But we should also be known for the way in which our witness leavens public life with a spirit of fairness, respect, restraint, and a search for common ground among contending positions. As you know, I have recently called for a Catholic Common Ground Project, a process of conversation and collaboration on issues that divide us within the Catholic Church. I do so not only because I believe we need such an initiative to enhance our own community but also because I believe that the style of our internal life is part of our public witness and contribution.

II. Justice and the Economy: A Catholic Perspective

One example of public religious witness, which attracted much attention a decade ago, was the pastoral letter on the U.S. economy, *Economic*

Justice for All. The tenth anniversary of the letter is being observed by a series of symposia, commemorations, and efforts to reflect upon what the pastoral letter's teaching on justice says to us in the new conditions of the 1990s. Since its publication ten years ago, the U.S. economy has continued to experience deep and far-reaching change generated by broader global patterns of economic interdependence. As bishops, we came to see in the 1980s that it was virtually impossible to isolate the U.S. economy for analysis apart from the global economy. Today, that truth is even more evident. Obviously many aspects of our economic life are quite positive: We are in a period of sustained economic growth, the competitiveness of American workers and industry has been demonstrated convincingly, the unemployment statistics are modest if not satisfactory, and inflation has been contained.

These "macro" indicators of our economic life are crucially important, but they do not address crucial **moral** questions that must be part of our assessment of U.S. economic life. While we have demonstrated our ability to compete internationally, not all in our nation have survived the competition. Economic dislocation, downsizing of major industries and loss of jobs, threats to familial and personal economic security are experiences all too well known by significant sectors of our population. The dynamic of the global market does not address the human costs of global competition either here or in other countries. The dynamic of the market must be complemented by a broader framework of social policy that attends to the needs of those who lose in the economic lottery.

The pastoral letter, *Economic Justice for All,* sought to focus the attention of both church and civil society on those whom our economic life has left out, left behind, and left alone. Catholic social and economic teaching is always concerned for the welfare of society as a whole and for the human dignity and human rights of each person; this systemic concern is exemplified in the concept of the common good. Within the context of a concern for all, however, there is a basic obligation to attend to the needs of the vulnerable—old or young, black or white, male or female. This is the religious mandate specified by the Hebrew prophets' call to protect "the orphans, the widows, and the resident aliens." It is the contemporary theme in Catholic teaching embodied in "the option for the poor." The striking fact is how accurately the prophets of 2700 years ago speak to our life today: Secular sources of analysis identify women and children as the most vulnerable groups in our society. Recent legislation—at the state and national level—effectively eliminates basic social support and services for "resident aliens" in our midst, whether they are legal or undocumented immigrants in our society. While pertinent **legal** distinctions exist among these two groups, the **moral** tradition of the prophets affirms moral obligations that we have to both, and uniquely to their children. The voices of the prophets are too accurate for us to be satisfied by "macro" indicators of economic health. The poor are still with us, and there is nothing in the Hebrew and Christian scriptures that tolerates complacency about their needs.

Two of our major socio-economic policy debates of the 1990s should make us think deeply about our societal contract, or conception of moral obligation among the citizens of this nation. Both the health care debate of the early 1990s and the welfare debate of this past year point to deeper issues than either health or welfare policy. The health care debate, large and complex as it was, contained a core element of the need to extend the social safety net to the 40 million citizens without basic coverage. The welfare debate, also complex in its elements, forced to the surface the question of whether any social safety net would be preserved at all. I should be clear: in highlighting the complexity of both policy issues, I acknowledge that health care policy must address the exponential increase in health care costs, the need to restructure parts of our delivery system, and the need to strike a balance between competing objectives of quality of care and the kinds of care provided in the health care system. I also acknowledge that reform of the welfare system is required for the good of all concerned: recipients, taxpayers, and providers.

Even with these considerations squarely before us, however, both of the extended policy debates on these issues, in my view, failed to meet basic standards of responsible policy. The leading industrial democracy in the world failed to extend a minimum standard of health care to its citizenry as a whole, and it has effectively dismantled the most basic protection for children in our society. Both the prophets and the pastoral letter stand in judgment of these actions. If this society cannot protect its most vulnerable—our sick and our children—it must be because we cannot think and speak clearly to each other about fundamental moral imperatives. Even in a deficit-driven economic debate, the fate of the sick and the young holds primacy of moral standing. Yes, we have "changed" health care and welfare. But from the perspective of those for whom we bear moral responsibility, change does not equal reform. It looks more like abandonment.

The deeper issues behind health care and welfare involve not only our societal compact with each other; they also involve allocation of responsibility for social policy that meets the standards of both effectiveness and justice. On a range of issues—social policy, tax policy, the stability of families, the cultivation of key values in personal and public life—I fear we are carrying on fundamental debates in a style that does not match in depth the substance of the issues addressed.

Running through most of our social policy debates is the discussion of the appropriate role of the state in our common life as a society. Catholic social thought is hardly statist in its premises or principles. The concept of "subsidiarity," a staple of Catholic social theory, explicitly requires that responses to social needs not start with the state. But subsidiarity does not yield a conception of the state that removes from it not only basic moral obligations for "the general welfare" but also specific moral duties toward those afflicted by illness, hardship, unemployment, and the lack of adequate nutrition and housing. My point is that it is not sufficient to carry on a discussion of the appropriate role of the state purely in terms of efficiency or size or "intrusiveness." These criteria are important but not significant if we omit a conception of what the state's moral role is in society. To speak of the state's moral role is not only to address the cultivation of moral standards; it also involves specific duties, often of a socio-economic nature, which the state has to its citizens.

Critics of this position will say I am making an abstract argument about the state's responsibility without acknowledging that the state does not generate the resources for its socio-economic policies and programs; citizens do that. The critics are partially right; we cannot discuss the moral obligations of the state apart from a substantive analysis of the obligations we have to each other as members of civil society. To the critics I will grant your point because I am convinced the deeper issue beneath our policy debates is precisely this question: how we conceive of our social bonds of obligation and responsibility, within families, beyond families to neighborhoods, and ultimately to the national community of which we are a part. A purely "contractual" view of our relationships is inadequate; it quickly reduces our obligations to those freely chosen, with no wider fabric of accountability. Contractual relations serve useful, limited functions, but we need a stronger fabric of social ties to undergird our life as a society. We require a sense of obligation to those we do not know, will never meet, and yet bear a responsibility for, precisely because of their need and our capacity to share in meeting that need.

There are many ways to express this stronger sense of social responsibility; John Paul II and the pastoral letter rely on the concept of "solidarity." Solidarity implies a fabric of moral bonds that exists among humans because of a shared sense of personhood. Solidarity precedes subsidiarity. The first defines our moral relationship; the second regulates how we will fulfill the duty of solidarity. Social solidarity finds expression in several ways. It sustains personal relationships; it binds families in a common life of love and support; it initiates and supports private efforts of charity and social service. But it also helps to define the moral responsibility of the state and its citizenry.

Solidarity points toward the neuralgic issue of U.S. politics: taxation. Taxes are one way in which the state facilitates our responsibilities to each other. Tax policy is a secular issue, but it is rooted in moral obligations we have to one another. A fair tax policy, one which obliges each of us to play a role in sustaining the human dignity of all in our society, is a requirement of distributive justice. In Catholic teaching, paying taxes is a virtue. Taxes help us to meet our pre-existing obligations to the poor.

In addition to establishing the basis for a just tax policy, Catholic teaching, I believe, has something critical to say to our contemporary debate about institutional responsibility and social policy. Over the last sixty years, three key ideas have characterized Catholic social teaching: subsidiarity, solidarity, and socialization. They need to be held in tandem: solidarity establishes the basis of common obligation; subsidiarity argues that private voluntary institutions are needed to fulfill our obligations; and socialization maintains that increased societal interdependence requires an activist state to meet the needs that private institutions cannot meet alone.[24] I spoke earlier about the need for new patterns of public-private collaboration. To address the deeper issues of our social policy debate we need to attend to these three concepts. We **do** have moral obligations to the vulnerable. So, we should have an adequate public policy to guarantee that the orphans, the widows, and the resident aliens are not left to the ravages of life.

As we seek to contribute to the societal debate about allocation of social responsibility, the role of our own social institutions becomes a crucial part of our public witness. Catholic schools, Catholic health care systems, and Catholic charities testify to our conviction that we have abiding social responsibilities. We live in a time of declining public resources and exploding public needs. Our institutions should not be used as an example that we do not need public engagement to meet social needs. But, as we argue for a strong fabric of social programs to meet human needs, our institutions can seek to demonstrate the quality of care for human life which a vision of human sacredness cultivates.

Precisely because we already support a broad range of social institutions, **and** because we are also committed in principle to an active if limited role for the state, the Catholic community should be a creative and articulate participant in the much-needed debate in this society about the comparative advantage that public institutions of the state have on **some** aspects of social policy and the severe liabilities they have on other issues. Seeking a new relationship of public and private agencies in our society is an imperative of the first order. Such a discussion involves constitutional issues of Church and state, societal issues of how best to structure civil society, and empirical issues of operational effectiveness. It is a far-reaching argument, but it must be undertaken because today too many suffer from the lack of an effective and humane policy vision.

III. The Sacredness of Life: Religion, Culture, and Politics

In this concluding section of my address, I return to the concept of the "Consistent Ethic." Thus far this afternoon, in addressing religion and politics, justice and economics, I have sought to reflect upon how we care for life in our midst, both personally and through public policy. Caring for life, supporting it, and responding to basic human needs of nutrition, health, housing, and education is an essential aspect of the "Consistent Ethic." As I have indicated, I believe we have yet a substantial way to go in caring for the lives of the least among us. But, in the contemporary U.S. context, **caring** for life does not exhaust our moral obligations. We now face in the 1990s profoundly threatening public issues where life **is being taken** without moral justification.

In proposing the "Consistent Ethic" over a decade ago, my purpose was to help create a dialogue about the full range of threats to life which modern society poses. I recognize the difference between the obligation to care for life and the obligation to defend life against attack. I recognize that the moral failure to care for life adequately is different from the moral crime of taking an innocent life. But I was convinced—and still am firmly convinced—that the overriding moral need in our society is to cultivate a conviction that we must face **all** the major threats to life, not only one or two. The "Consistent Ethic" precisely seeks to relate our moral analysis about **different** kinds of moral problems. It seeks to provide a framework within which individuals and groups, who begin with a concern for one moral dimension of life, can be brought to see the threat posed by other issues in our societies.

When we shift our focus in U.S. society from thinking about **caring** for life to **defending** life, there is hardly a better guide than Pope John Paul II's encyclical, *The Gospel of Life*. The Holy Father identified three issues—abortion, capital punishment, and euthanasia—in his sweeping critique of what he described as a creeping "culture of death." Here again, even within the Catholic tradition these three issues have not been simply collapsed into one question. Capital punishment has not in the past been regarded as "unjust killing" in the way abortion and euthanasia have been. But the power of the papal argument is that it helps us to see that, today, different kinds of taking life should be systematically related. Faced with a need to build a societal consensus that respects life, Catholic teaching has clearly moved to restrict the state's right to take life, even in instances previously approved.

There is an inner logic to an ethic that respects life and a contrary logic in quick, frequent resort to solving problems by taking life. While not seeking to simplify complex human problems, I suggest we think carefully about our society, which today sustains 1.5 million abortions, which is overwhelmingly in favor of capital punishment, and which is now moving rapidly toward acceptance of assisted suicide. Each of these problems must be argued on its own terms. There are clearly distinctions among positions held across this spectrum of issues, but there is also a truth to be learned in relating these three questions. The truth is that respect for life will cost us something. To move beyond solutions to problems by taking life will require a more expansive care for life—at its beginning and its end.

I cannot plunge at this point in my address into a detailed assessment of these three issues in our public life. But I do think that relating the experience we have had on abortion to the current debate about assisted suicide can be helpful. Once again, the deeper themes behind the specific choices are the most important ones. In both the abortion and the assisted-suicide debates, I am convinced that the basic picture one has of the social fabric of life is crucial to how one makes a moral judgment on the specific issues.

The abortion debate has been publicly framed as a "private choice." In both public debate and recent judicial decisions, assisted suicide has been argued in similarly "private" terms. Such a construction of these questions promotes the idea that social consequences are lacking in both cases. I am convinced that such a view is profoundly short-sighted. To use assisted suicide as an example, it **is** undoubtedly a deeply personal issue because it touches upon life and death, and a person's conception of whom they are accountable to in life and death. But it also directly affects the doctor–patient relationship and, through that, the wider role of doctors in our society. As has been noted by others, it threatens to introduce a deep ambiguity into the very definition of medical care, if care comes to involve killing. Beyond the physician, a move to assisted suicide and, perhaps beyond that, to euthanasia creates social ambiguity about the law. In civilized society the law exists to protect life. When it also begins to legitimate the taking of life as a policy, one has a right to ask what lies ahead for our life together as a society. There are deep psychological, social, and moral questions at stake in how we conceive our social relationship to each other and particularly to the most vulnerable in our society—again the very young and the very sick become test cases.

After two decades of struggle over abortion, our society and our church now face a double challenge to defend life even as we continue to pursue ways to care for and nurture it. I remain convinced that our witness will be more effective, more persuasive, and better equipped to address the moral challenge we face, if we witness to life across the spectrum of life from conception until natural death, calling our society to see the connection between caring for life and defending it.

Here again, there are implications for the internal life of the Church. It is urgently necessary that we remain a voice for life—vigorous, strong, consistent. In the recent case of partial birth abortion, the protest raised from within our Church and by others was absolutely necessary. The procedure should not be allowed; it should have been stopped. There will undoubtedly be other cases, at both ends of life, when our voice, our advocacy, our legitimate efforts will be needed.

But we also must continue to witness by deed to a conception of caring for life that seeks to invite the wider society to see the linkage between care for and defense of life. So, I commend those who have been organized in support of single mothers, those who seek to provide a place for pregnant women of all ages to receive support and care, those who sponsor and serve in health care facilities and programs that care for the dying and sustain hope even in the face of a long, painful dying process. These efforts from within the Church are essential to match the public witness of the Church in society.

Conclusion

As you are well aware, this has been a long lecture. In bringing it to a close, I will consciously change its tone and tenor. When I accepted Father

O'Donovan's invitation, I undertook the assignment of giving a policy lecture suited for an academic audience. I have tried to fulfill that task this afternoon. But I also thought at the time of the invitation that I would likely have several opportunities to contribute to the U.S. debate on religion and our public life, on the moral values of human dignity and the sacredness of human life.

As you are aware, I now face a very different horizon. In human terms, I have been advised my life span is now quite limited. This fact does not change any of the moral or social analysis which I have used in this address. But it does shape one perspective decisively. I have already said that, as a person of faith—of resurrection faith—I see death as a friend not a foe, and the experience of death is, I am convinced, a transition from life to life—from grace to glory, as St. Augustine said.

These are my deepest convictions of faith, which has been rooted in God's word and confirmed by the sacraments of the Church. But the experience I am now going through sheds new light on the moral order also. As a bishop, I have tried, in season and out of season, to shape and share a moral message about the unique value of human life and our common responsibilities for it. As my life now slowly ebbs away, as my temporal destiny becomes clearer each hour and each day, I am not anxious, but rather reconfirmed in my conviction about the wonder of human life, a gift that flows from the very being of God and is entrusted to each of us. It is easy in the rush of daily life or in its tedium to lose the sense of wonder that is appropriate to this gift. It is even easier at the level of our societal relations to count some lives as less valuable than others, especially when caring for them costs us—financially, emotionally, or in terms of time, effort, and struggle.

The truth is, of course, that each life is of infinite value. Protecting and promoting life—caring for it and defending it—is a complex task in social and policy terms. I have struggled with the specifics often and have sensed the limits of reason in the struggle to know the good and do the right. My final hope is that my efforts have been faithful to the truth of the gospel of life and that you and others like you will find in this gospel the vision and strength needed to promote and nurture the great gift of life God has shared with us.

Faithful and Hopeful: The Catholic Common Ground Project

October 24, 1996

Two and a half months ago, I announced an initiative called the **Catholic Common Ground Project**. My aim was to help Catholics address, creatively and faithfully, questions that are vital if the Church in the United States is to flourish as we enter the next millennium. At every level, we needed, I felt, to move beyond the distrust, the polarization, and the entrenched positions that have hampered our responses.

At the same time, I released a statement, *"Called to Be Catholic: Church in a Time of Peril."*[25] Its very first paragraph summed up what this initiative was about: "Will the Catholic Church in the United States enter the new millennium as a Church of promise," it asked, or as "a Church on the defensive"? The outcome, it proposed, depended on "whether American Catholicism can confront an array of challenges with honesty and imagination." "American Catholics," it stated, "must reconstitute the conditions for addressing our differences constructively." This can happen if we find a common ground. But not just any common ground. It has to be, as the statement said, "a common ground centered on faith in Jesus, marked by accountability to the living Catholic tradition, and ruled by a renewed spirit of civility, dialogue, generosity, and broad and serious consultation."

At that time, I also announced that I had assembled a committee of outstanding Catholics to join me in this Project—seven other bishops, including a fellow Cardinal, five priests, three women religious, and eight lay men and women. They come from across the country, from diverse backgrounds in public service, intellectual life, business, and labor—and from a range of viewpoints regarding the needs of the Church.

Although I felt that the statement *"Called to Be Catholic"* was an excellent description of our situation today, I did not ask these advisors to endorse its every word. I regret that some press reports mistakenly

158

reported that committee members had signed the statement. My conviction, in fact, was that the words were not enough. The idea behind the Catholic Common Ground Project was to demonstrate how this call for a civil and generous dialogue, Christ-centered and accountable to the Church's living tradition and teaching of the authentic magisterium, could be put into action.

To do that will take time, and at the end of August, as you well know, I discovered how little time remains for me personally. Earlier today, I met with the committee so that my role in this venture can be passed to others, and, this evening I am sharing these reflections with you in the hope that that you too, in your own ways, will take up this task.

My thoughts this evening will cover several areas: the response to the Project, the reality of differences in the Church, the relationship of the Project to doctrine and dissent, what is meant by the word "dialogue," and, finally, my hopes for the future of the Project.

Response

The importance of our task has been reinforced by the response that the announcement of the **Catholic Common Ground Project** has generated. I am not thinking so much of the public statements, for and against, that were widely reported in the media, although those, too, were welcome and valuable, even when unanticipated.

Rather, I am thinking of the outpouring of personal letters that have been sent to me and to the National Pastoral Life Center in New York—letters filled with words like "grateful," "heartening," "timely," "common sense," and even "joy." Priests and parishioners, women and men, recounted their frustrations and their fears that hope for the Church was fading into deadlock or acrimony. Their letters also offered ideas, energy, institutional support. They reported discussions already being organized around *"Called to be Catholic."* The letters were charged with the sense that something bottled up had been released, that something grown dormant was being reawakened.

Most of the letters avoided any note of triumphalism. They called, instead, for humility and prayerful reflection. Among the letter writers were some identifying themselves as conservatives and others calling themselves liberals, but both confessing that they had felt the acids of polarization, anger, and overreaction at work in their own souls.

There were, however, exceptions. A few people welcomed the Project, it seemed, as offering a new front or a promising arena in what they clearly viewed as little more than an ongoing battle within the Church. But most, I am happy to say, seemed truly to feel the need to apply to themselves as well as to others the statement's call that we examine our situation with fresh eyes, open minds, and changed hearts.

If there was any frequent misunderstanding of the Catholic Common Ground Project, both among its supporters and its critics, it only reflected the Church's current state of nervous anxiety. Some people hoped, and others feared, that this initiative would aim ambitiously at resolving all the Church's major conflicts in our nation. Some seemed to imagine that the project planned to bring contending sides, like labor-management negotiators, to a bargaining table and somehow hammer out a new consensus on contentious issues within the Church. In this misconception, the Common Ground Project's conferences would culminate in quasi-official reports or recommendations that had the potential to challenge or supplant the authority of diocesan bishops.

I apologize if any of my statements contributed to this impression. Precisely because this effort is so important to the hopes of so many, we need to be clear about the limits of this effort. Our aim is not to resolve all our differences or to establish a new ecclesial structure. Rather, it is, first of all, to learn how to make our differences fruitful. Agreements may emerge—all the better. But our first step is closer to what John Courtney Murray called the hard task of achieving genuine disagreement.

Common ground, in this sense, is not a new set of conclusions. It is a way of exploring our differences. It is a common spirit and ethic of dialogue. It is a space of trust set within boundaries. It is a place of respect where we can explore our differences, assured in the understanding that neither is everything "cut-and-dried" nor is everything "up for grabs."

Differences

As we know, differences have always existed in the Church. St. Paul's letters and the Acts of the Apostles and the fact that there are four gospel accounts rather than one all tell us that Christian unity has always coexisted with Christian differences. Differences are the natural reflection of our diversity, a diversity that comes with catholicity. Differences are the natural consequence of our grappling with a divine mystery that always remains beyond our complete comprehension. And differences, it must be added, can also spring from human sinfulness.

In the Church's history, differences have often been the seedbeds of our most profound understanding of God and salvation. Differences and dissatisfaction have spurred extraordinary institutional creativity. And differences too often have provoked unnecessary, wasteful, and sometimes terrible, division.

What about today? By most historical standards the Catholic Church is not racked by overt divisions. Quite the contrary. No other global movement or body—political, religious, ideological—begins to approach the unity demonstrated time and again in the travels of the Holy Father whose remarkable pastoral leadership as shepherd and teacher has prepared us well for the new millennium and can be a helpful basis for the dialogue about which I will speak later. Our oneness in Spirit, our gathering from east to west at the eucharistic banquet, has never been rendered so visible to the human eye.

Yet, we have learned that in modern societies the greatest dangers may not manifest themselves so much in schism and rebellion as in hemorrhage and lassitude, complacency, the insidious draining of vitality, the haughty retreat into isolation, the dispiriting pressure of retrenchment. Secularization has triumphed where the Church defaulted.

Are the differences among U.S. Catholics generating reflection, exchange, debate, ideas, initiative, decisiveness? Or are they producing distrust, polemics, weariness, withdrawal, inertia, deadlock?

No one can answer these questions definitively. But I and many others representing a range of theological outlooks feel that, in far too many cases, the brave new sparks and steady flame of vitality in the Church are being smothered by the camps and distractions of our quarrels. The statement *"Called to Be Catholic"* described the situation realistically. "For three decades," it noted, "the Church has been divided by different responses to the Second Vatican Council and to the tumultuous years that followed."

Despite the emergence of new generations with new questions, experiences, and needs, the statement continued, "Party lines have hardened. A mood of suspicion and acrimony hangs over many of those most active in the Church's life . . . One consequence is that many of us are refusing to acknowledge disquieting realities, perhaps fearing that they may reflect poorly on our past efforts or arm our critics . . . Candid discussion is inhibited . . . Ideas, journals, and leaders are pressed to align themselves with preexisting camps."

One could expand on that analysis. Rather than listen to an idea, we look for its "worst case" extension; we suspect a hidden agenda.

Anticipating attack, we avoid self-criticism and fear frank evaluation. We silence our doubts. We list the events of ecclesial life in parallel columns as wins or losses in a kind of zero-sum game.

I am almost embarrassed to give examples—first, because some of them are so painfully obvious and, second, because it is difficult to do so without inviting this process of testing for partisanship and hidden agendas. But let me mention only the very first item among the statement's examples of urgent questions that the Church needs to address openly and honestly: "the changing roles of women." That would seem to be a rather obvious topic for examination, since the Holy Father has himself drawn our attention to it. Yet in the public responses to the statement, the fact that this question was listed first was enough to render our undertaking suspect by some, while the fact that it did not stipulate anything about ordination was a cause for rejection by others.

I believe that we long for a climate where a question as basic as this could be brought to the table in a mood of good will and with a readiness to learn from one another. We long to exchange ideas, informed by Church teaching and witness, with a confidence that our heartfelt concerns for living the gospel faithfully will be heard and not slighted or betrayed.

Catholic Doctrine

Do the differences on topics like this have to do with Catholic doctrine, an area that is obviously less subject to change than pastoral practice? The question is significant. Some of the harshest criticisms of the Catholic Common Ground Project have arisen from anxiety that the exploration of differences could compromise the truth of Catholic doctrine. Such doctrine, it is said, already constitutes more than sufficient common ground, if only it were proclaimed without trepidation.

The answer to this question is twofold. First, many of the controversial differences among U.S. Catholics are not strictly doctrinal but, indeed, pastoral. The collaboration between clergy and laity in parish life, the effectiveness of religious education, the quality of liturgical celebration, the means of coping with declining numbers of priests and sisters—all the crucial areas pose numerous questions for which neither the *Catechism of the Catholic Church* nor the documents of Vatican II nor other magisterial sources provide precise and authoritative answers.

For example, in what sequence, and with what mixture of the affective and the conceptual, should the truths of the faith be introduced to children? How should religious education be structured around family life, sacramental preparation, classroom activities, the liturgy and its cycles? How should resources be distributed among Catholic schools, other forms of religious education, the family teaching moments of baptism, First Communion, marriage, and death? How should religious educators be formed, and programs realistically suited to volunteer teachers with high turnover rates? How can qualified lay professionals be identified, selected, sustained, and assured of respect and recompense in team ministries? What can be done to make the quality of homilies and congregational singing genuine assets in building a parish community?

To no small extent, the future vitality of the Church hangs on such issues, and for concrete solutions we will not be able to rely solely on magisterial documents but will, instead, have to use our collective wisdom, knowledge, prudence, and sense of priorities.

But that is not the complete answer. There are doctrinal aspects to even the most pastoral of these questions, and these doctrinal aspects generate anxiety. It is both justified and imperative to ask what are the implications for doctrine of pastoral proposals or the implications for pastoral proposals of doctrine.

To ask such questions is more than an obligation. It is also an opportunity. Catholic doctrine provides enduring truths about divine and human reality. It should enlighten our minds, guide our daily actions, inform our spiritual striving. As we know, doctrine is often refined and nuanced, and is expressed as a carefully articulated structure rather than as an undifferentiated block. There also exists, as the Second Vatican Council stated, and the Catechism repeats, a "hierarchy" of truths varying in their relation to the foundation of Christian faith. And Catholic belief is not static. Assisted by the Holy Spirit, the Church is able to grow in its understanding of the heritage of faith. The *Catechism of the Catholic Church* is a gift to the Church because it is a compendium of this rich doctrinal heritage as it has developed over the centuries.

What is the practical import of this interlacing of the pastoral and the doctrinal? On the one hand, as *"Called to Be Catholic"* urges, "We should not rush to interpret disagreements as conflicts of starkly opposing principles rather than as differences in degree or in prudential pastoral judgments about the relevant facts." On the other hand, we must also "detect the valid insights and worries" embedded in our differing arguments. That being said, ultimately, our reflections and deliberations must be accountable to Scripture and tradition authentically interpreted—or in the words of the statement, to "the cloud of witnesses over the centuries or the living magisterium of the Church exercised by the bishops and the Chair of Peter." On this point let there be no uncertainty!

Dissent

You may have noticed that so far I have spoken about differences without using the word "dissent." Some people have objected that the Catholic Common Ground Project will legitimate dissent, and others, perhaps, have hoped that it will. In part, I have addressed this concern by noting the range of differences among U.S. Catholics that are not strictly or primarily doctrinal. But dissent, in addition, is a complicated term. I mean neither to avoid it nor to pretend to address all the issues surrounding it.

One can find, however, some major points of consensus about dissent.

On the one hand, consider the view that all public disagreement or criticism of Church teaching is illegitimate. Such an unqualified understanding is unfounded and would be a disservice to the Church. "Room must be made for responsible dissent in the Church," writes Father Avery Dulles, whom no one can accuse of being radical or reckless in his views. "Theology always stands under correction."

"Dissent should neither be glorified nor be vilified," Father Dulles adds. It inevitably risks weakening the Church as a sign of unity, but it can nonetheless be justified, and to suppress it would be harmful. "The good health of the Church demands continual revitalization by new ideas," Father Dulles says, adding that "nearly every creative theologian has at one time or another been suspected of corrupting the faith." In fact, according to Dulles, theologians ought to alert Church authorities to the shortcomings of its teachings.[26]

Similarly, in *Veritatis Splendor* Pope John Paul II distinguished between "limited and occasional dissent" and "an overall and systematic calling into question of traditional moral doctrine."[27] I would argue that dissent ceases to be legitimate when it takes the form of aggressive public campaigns against Church teachings that undermine the authority of the magisterium itself.

No one can deny that such campaigns exist. But I would go further. The problem of dissent today is not so much the voicing of serious criticism but the popularity of dismissive, demagogic, "cute" commentary, dwelling on alleged motives, exploiting stereotypes, creating stock villains, employing reliable "laugh lines." The kind of responsible disagreement of which I speak must not include "caricatures" that "undermine the Church as a community of faith" by assuming Church authorities to be "generally ignorant, self-serving, and narrow-minded." It takes no more than a cursory reading of the more militant segments of the Catholic press, on both ends of the theological and ideological spectrum, to reveal how widespread, and how corrosive, such caricatures have become.

This is why the Catholic Common Ground Project, while affirming "legitimate debate, discussion, and diversity," specifically targets "pop scholarship, sound-bite theology, unhistorical assertions, and flippant dismissals." Moreover, it aims at giving Catholics another model for exploring our differences. Before speaking of that model I want to make it clear that, in speaking of a "common ground," this Project does not aim at the lowest common denominator. Nor when it speaks of dialogue does it imply compromise. Rather, in both instances its goal is the fullest possible understanding of and internalization of the truth.

Dialogue

The Project's model is dialogue. But we have done more than merely invoke that word. Unfortunately, the call for dialogue has too often become routine, a gambit in the wars of imagemaking, a tactic in reopening or prolonging bureaucratic negotiations. Nonetheless the recognition and highlighting of dialogue remains one of the glories of the Second Vatican Council and of the papacies that nurtured and followed it. In dialogue we affirm, examine, deepen, and rectify our own defining beliefs in relationship to another person. That relationship involves opposition but also sincere respect, trust, and expectation of mutual enrichment.

The statement *"Called to Be Catholic"* proposes conditions for a renewed and successful dialogue among U.S. Catholics. Let us remind ourselves of a few of them:

1. that Jesus Christ, present in Scripture and sacrament, be central to all that we do;
2. that we reaffirm basic truths and stand accountable to Scripture and Catholic tradition, witnessed and conveyed to us by the Spirit-filled, living Church and its magisterium exercised by the bishops and the Chair of Peter;
3. that the complexity and richness of this tradition not be reduced or ignored by fundamentalist appeals to a text or a decree or by narrow appeals to individual or contemporary experience;

4. that the Church be treated not as a merely human organization but as a communion, a spiritual family, requiring that a hermeneutic of suspicion be balanced by a hermeneutic of love and retrieval, and that Catholic leadership embrace wide and serious consultation;

5. that our discussions assume the need for boundaries, distinctions, and defining limits, even where these may be open to reexamination;

6. that we recognize no single group as possessing a monopoly on solutions to the Church's problems or the right to spurn the mass of Catholics and their leaders as unfaithful;

7. that we test proposals for pastoral realism;

8. that we presume those with whom we differ to be in good faith and put the best possible construction on their positions;

9. that, above all, we keep the liturgy, our common worship, from becoming a battleground for confrontation and polarization.

Hopes

I trust that these reflections have been of some help in our coming to a better understanding of the Project and its direction. Now allow me some personal thoughts.

Shortly after the Project was announced, a friend asked me, "Joe, why at this time in your life did you take on this Project?" My friend was referring to the stress of the last three years, in particular the stress of a false accusation and then of being a cancer patient. It was a good question. It prompted me to reflect more deeply about my many life experiences and my own spiritual journey.

I thought immediately of the lessons I had learned from my mentors, Archbishop Paul Hallinan of Atlanta and John Cardinal Dearden of Detroit: to trust that, through open and honest dialogue, differences could be resolved and the gospel proclaimed in its integrity. Over the years I learned from you and so many other of our sisters and brothers the correctness of what these two great churchmen taught me. I have been impressed and humbled by the willingness of so many to rise above differences in search for the truth that can bind us together. I have been nurtured by the peace and joy of communities that have worked hard for reconciliation and peace.

This same insight prompted me to move beyond the family of faith and speak to our society about a consistent ethic of life. In asking opponents of abortion and opponents of capital punishment and nuclear war to perceive a whole spectrum of life-issues not in identical terms but, rather, in relationship to one another, I have been moved by the conviction that the Church's understanding of the gospel defies conventional political and ideological lines. By juxtaposing positions that are conventionally set apart and by searching for the common thread, we enrich our own understanding and open others to persuasion.

Similarly, the Catholic Common Ground Project offers the promise of our rising above hardened party lines and finding renewal in the splendor of the truth revealed in the person of Jesus who is our Lord and our savior.

This evening, I assure you that, having entered the final phase of my life's journey, I am even more committed than before to this central conviction. A dying person does not have time for the peripheral or the accidental. He or she is drawn to the essential, the important—yes, the eternal. And what is important, my friends, is that we find that unity with the Lord and within the community of faith for which Jesus prayed so fervently on the night before he died. To say it quite boldly, it is wrong to waste the precious gift of the time given to us, as God's chosen servants, on acrimony and division.

And so, in that spirit I hand on to you the gift that was given to me—a vision of the Church that trusts in the power of the Spirit so much that it can risk authentic dialogue. I hand that gift on to you without fear or trepidation. I say this because I know that it is a gift you already prize and cherish. I ask you, without waiting and on your own, to strengthen the common ground, to examine our situation with fresh eyes, open minds, and changed hearts, and to confront our challenges with honesty and imagination. Guided by the Holy Spirit, together, we can more effectively respond to the challenges of our times as we carry forward the mission that the Lord Jesus gave to us, his disciples. It is to promote that mission that the constructive dialogue we seek is so important.

In addition, I ask you to read carefully *"Called to Be Catholic."* Like some of the Committee, you may not agree with every sentence or paragraph. But ask yourself carefully where and why you agree or disagree. Discuss it in your families, your parishes, your schools. Make it the occasion for a serious examination of conscience and not for further contention.

Then, I ask you to go a step further. Whether you are guided by this statement or similar principles, please decide how it might modify the conduct or the tone of whatever group efforts engage you in the

Church—your parish council, your prayer group, your Catholic grade school or high school faculty, your academic department or professional organization if these deal with religious issues. Are these the principles—the centrality of Jesus, the serious accountability to Church tradition and authentic teaching, the spirit of dialogue and consultation—that govern the Catholic periodicals you read, the television programs you watch, the organizations to which you belong, or the conferences you attend? If not, make your preferences known.

As you do this, return to the teachings of the Second Vatican Council, which I believe with all my being was the work of God's Holy Spirit. While there is so much in conciliar teaching that can guide these efforts, you might find inspiration in a passage at the close of *Gaudium et Spes,* the Pastoral Constitution on the Church in the Modern World. This passage calls on the Church to become a sign of sincere dialogue as part of its mission to enlighten the world with the gospel's message and unite all people in the one Spirit. I close with the inspiring words of that passage: "Such a mission," the Council fathers instructed, "requires us first of all to create in the Church itself mutual esteem, reverence and harmony, and acknowledge all legitimate diversity; in this way all who constitute the one people of God will be able to engage in ever more fruitful dialogue, whether they are pastors or other members of the faithful. For the ties which unite the faithful together are stronger than those which separate them: let there be unity in what is necessary, freedom in what is doubtful, and charity in everything."[28]

Endnotes

The editor has provided the following notes to document and explicate various aspects of the addresses by Cardinal Bernardin.

1. National Conference of Catholic Bishops, *The Challenge of Peace: God's Promise and Our Response* (Washington, D.C.: United States Catholic Conference, 1983), par. 186.

2. *Ibid.*, par. 187.

3. The MX missile system was conceived as a mode for basing intercontinental ballistic missiles that would make them mobile and so would enhance their chances of surviving a first strike or surprise attack by the Soviet Union. It was seen by its proponents as a way to increase the stability of the deterrent and by its critics as an enormously costly and potentially destabilizing system. It encountered serious political opposition, especially in those western states where it would have been deployed. It was eventually eliminated in the course of arms control negotiations in the Bush Administration, when the terms of superpower relations had changed well beyond the expectations of participants in the earlier policy debates.

4. Jose Napoleon Duarte, a graduate of the University of Notre Dame and the leader of the Christian Democratic party, served as president of El Salvador from 1984 to 1989.

5. Catholic Bishops of Nicaragua, "Easter 1984 Pastoral Letter," *Origins* 14, 9 (July 26, 1984), pp. 131–4.

6. National Conference of Catholic Bishops, *The Challenge of Peace*, par. 234.

7. John Paul II, "1982 World Day of Peace Message," *Origins* 11, 30 (January 7, 1982), p. 476, par. 6.

8. National Conference of Catholic Bishops, *The Challenge of Peace*, par. 19.

9. John Courtney Murray, S.J. (1904–1967), professor of theology at Woodstock College and editor of *Theological Studies* (1941–1967), contributed greatly to the shaping of *Dignitatis humanae*, the decree of Vatican II on religious liberty.

10. The *Didache*, a summary of Christian teaching dating from the late first century and recovered in 1883, has been described by Johannes Quasten as "the most important document of the subapostolic period and the oldest source of ecclesiastical law which we possess." *Patrology* (Utrecht: Spectrum, 1963), Vol. I, p. 30.

11. John Ford, S.J., "The Morality of Obliteration Bombing," *Theological Studies* 5 (1944), pp. 261–309.

12. Bishop James Malone, "Statement of October 14, 1984," *Origins* 14, 9 (October 25, 1984), p. 291.

13. Eventually published as "A Report on *The Challenge of Peace* and Policy Developments 1983–1988," *Origins* 18, 9 (July 21, 1988), pp. 133–48.

14. "It's Over, Debbie," *Journal of the American Medical Association* 259 (January 8, 1988), p. 272.

15. See the third draft of *The Challenge of Peace*, in *Origins* 12, 44 (April 14, 1983), p. 715. The contrast between "halt" and "curb" was widely construed as indicating different attitudes to the widely discussed proposal for a "freeze" on the development and deployment of nuclear weapons systems. The second draft of the pastoral letter on peace (October 1982) called for "support for immediate bilateral verifiable agreements to halt the testing, production, and deployment of new strategic weapons," in *Origins* 12, 10 (October 28, 1982), p. 317. This was widely thought to constitute an endorsement of the "nuclear freeze" proposal that had considerable popular appeal. Largely at the insistence of Archbishop (later Cardinal) John O'Connor of New York, the language of this section was changed in the third draft of the letter to call for "support for immediate bilateral verifiable agreements to curb the testing, production, and deployment of new nuclear weapons"; in *Origins* 12, 44 (April 14, 1983), p. 715. The language of the third draft stands in the final version of *The Challenge of Peace*, par. 191. A vivid, though somewhat partisan, account of the maneuverings within the bishops' committee that was preparing the document and of the efforts of the Reagan administration to influence the outcome can be found in Jim Castelli, *The Bishops and the Bomb* (Garden City, N.Y.: Doubleday, 1983), esp. pp. 137–41.

16. National Conference of Catholic Bishops, *The Challenge of Peace*, par. 186.

17. John Paul II, Letter to International Seminar on the Moral Implications of a Nuclear Conflict, August 23, 1982; cited in *The Challenge of Peace*, par. 176.

18. Vatican II, *Gaudium et spes*, Pastoral Constitution on the Church in the Modern World, par. 79, approves the legal recognition of conscientious objection to military service.

19. United States Catholic Conference Administrative Board, "Humanitarian Nightmare," Statement of March 25, 1993, *Origins* 22, 43 (April 8, 1993), pp. 735–6.

20. The text of the resolution can be found in *Origins* 23, 7 (July 1, 1993), 97–102.

21. U.S. Catholic Bishops, "Pastoral Letter on Health and Health Care," *Origins* 11, 25 (December 3, 1987), p. 402.

22. Philip Keane, S.S., *Health Care Reform: A Catholic View* (New York: Paulist, 1993), p. 134.

23. In 1996, the United States Supreme Court agreed to consider two federal appeals court decisions that had overturned Washington's and New York's bans on physician-assisted suicide. At issue in both cases was the existence of a constitutional right to end one's life. The case provoked wide public discussion, and many "friends of the court" briefs were filed with the Supreme Court. In June 1997, the Supreme Court unanimously overturned the federal court decisions thereby reinstating the state bans on assisted suicide. The text of the letter is taken from *Origins* 26, 25 (December 5, 1996), p. 412.

24. "Socialization" is to be understood along the lines of John XXIII's encyclical, *Mater et Magistra* (1961), pars. 59–67, in which the pope discusses the "increase in social relationships" which is characteristic of contemporary society and which has both positive and negative aspects. Some early translations of the document translated the Latin as calling for "increased socialization." That this does not mean increased government ownership of the means of production is clear from the fact that John XXIII clearly rejects socialism in *Mater et Magistra,* par. 34.

25. Catholic Common Ground Project, "Called to Be Catholic: Church in a Time of Peril," *Origins* 26, 11 (August 29, 1996), pp. 165–70.

26. Avery Dulles, S.J., *The Craft of Theology* (New York: Crossroad 1992), pp. 169–170.

27. John Paul II, *Veritatis splendor.*

28. Vatican II, *Gaudium et spes*, Pastoral Constitution on the Church in the Modern World, par. 92.

Index